THE RENAISSANCE CAMPAIGN

THE RENAISSANCE CAMPAIGN

A PROBLEM-SOLVING FORMULA FOR YOUR BIGGEST CHALLENGES

JOHN ROGERS

LIONCREST
PUBLISHING

THE RENAISSANCE CAMPAIGN
A Problem-Solving Formula for Your Biggest Challenges

ISBN   978-1-5445-1154-2 *Hardcover*
         978-1-5445-1153-5 *Paperback*
         978-1-5445-1152-8 *Ebook*

To Margaret and Buck, who bestowed upon me a right brain/left brain view of life. To Diane as well, who's rafted the river of life with me, and I'm so much richer for it.

CONTENTS

INTRODUCTION

What was isn't.

What is wasn't.

What will be is a multifaceted glimmer.

Disruption is everywhere.

It interrupts and destabilizes our systems and norms, impacting individuals, organizations, and indeed, all of our society. We face cultural, environmental, and technological disruptions on a daily basis. Rarely do we recognize them before they slap us in the face, either because we try to ignore them, or because we simply don't see them coming until it's too late.

The more technology advances, the faster change occurs,

and the easier it becomes to proliferate information, deluging our world with so much noise, it's a wonder we haven't all gone deaf.

We are drowning in data, and the amount of new information we're expected to absorb each day is unmanageable without methodologies in place.

These disruptions have become staples of our lives, the rapid rate of societal change often hindering progress rather than helping it. Decision-makers in every field can barely keep up with today's challenges, much less plan and prepare for tomorrow. Navigating it all feels like sprinting through a labyrinth.

Our challenges are not limited in scope either. They are as small as figuring out how you're going to squeeze in grocery shopping this week when every minute already seems accounted for. They are as stressful as figuring out how to take your small business to a medium-sized one without compromising your family time. They are as enormous as being the head of a multibillion-dollar organization that answers to shareholders but has an equal responsibility to take care of its workforce.

Trying to figure this out without a process in place can feel like trudging through muck versus gliding through your "hero's journey" as the main character in your movie called *Life*. At times, the journey is filled with pitfalls and setbacks that seem insurmountable, and the challenges laid before you can get pushed into a box labeled "too hard" because you lack an executable solution set to resolve them. Yet within every hero's journey there are eye-opening moments that will guide you through the darkness, changed for the better, with a new approach and mindset.

Two such approaches are holistic thinking and campaigns, which provide the backbone of this book. They lend themselves to a strategy that will help you overcome the many obstacles you face—that will allow you to move them from the "too hard" box to the "to solve" box, and then show you how to solve them and, quite simply, how to get shit done.

The truth in all of this is that no matter how big or small your challenges, there are ways to manage the disruptions of our world, but we need tools to do so—tools I've discovered through failure, through success, and, of all places, in fifteenth-century Italy.

LOOK TO THE PAST TO SOLVE THE PRESENT

It was Florence, twenty-first century, though for all I knew, I could have fallen into the 1400s. The city's rooftops were crimson red, its stone ancient, stories buried in their fissures.

I'd just spent the past few weeks biking and eating my way through Italy with my wife, marveling at the enormity of the Colosseum, the splendor of the Vatican, the serenity of Tuscany's careening hills, and now Florence.

The city was beautiful, sure.

But that's not what captivated me.

Florence embodied ingenuity and forward thinking at a time when everyone was backward. It embodied holistic thinking, which we need today more than ever. Vestiges of such brilliance remind at every corner. You don't need to visit the Leonardo da Vinci Museum or the Palazzo Medici Riccardi to appreciate that this city was once an epicenter of cultural change embracing vast disciplines of thought.

This was the city that created the Renaissance.

This book isn't about the Renaissance, and it isn't about Florence. I'm no expert in either, but I am inspired by them.

It's a book about thinking and doing—big difficult things worth doing, sure, but also making day-to-day life more navigable and manageable.

The first people in recent history to encapsulate this mentality were those born out of the Renaissance. Responsible for both instigating the movement and responding to the swell of humanism and interconnected thinking sweeping through Europe, the Renaissance greats cultivated a new methodology of thinking we still use, albeit unconsciously, to this day. (To pay homage to the Renaissance greats is to bow to the Greeks, for classic history inspired their movement, but for the sake of simplicity, we will remain in fourteenth- to sixteenth-century Italy and England.)

As we today are drowning in technology and data, they then were drowning in pages. Johannes Gutenberg's invention of the printing press in 1439 revolutionized the written word. In the Middle Ages, information flowed directly from the church and nobility to the people, so the masses had to rely on others for their information. The Gutenberg press changed that. Reading was no longer for the elite. The widespread distribution of texts bolstered a brand-new middle class and, for the first time, allowed for a true convergence of thinking across disciplines. People were beginning to think for themselves in a way society had never permitted. It created a renaissance—a rebirth—that shifted the foundations of cities across Europe, permanently altering the course of history.

A NEW APPROACH

The invention of the computer chip and then the internet spurred a shift analogous to what Gutenberg procured with the printing press.

Data and news used to stem from a finite number of sources, with the rate of progress moderate enough to learn, assimilate, and adapt before the next massive disruption. This is no longer the case. It hasn't been the case for years.

Now, anybody with a computer and access to the internet can supply their own content. (Whether that content is truthful or factual is an entirely different challenge.) Thus, the vertical means by which we used to receive information has fundamentally changed. Today, it can be vertical, horizontal, circular, linear, and nonlinear. As the adage goes, knowledge is power, and access to information grants such power. Today, more than ever before, people can access information and fact-check sources in a manner that alters the hierarchies of society.

The digital age certainly recalls the fifteenth century's transcendental shift of how people navigated society; whether we revert to the dark ages or spur a new Renaissance remains to be seen. Unlike during the times of da Vinci, we seem to have become more inundated with information yet less deferential toward the importance of facts and holistic thinking.

And it's a problem.

The challenge is that the old way of solving diverse problem sets no longer works. Organizations and individuals need an additional way of thinking about things, an additional way of approaching challenges, and a model to ensure that they can execute effectively through it all. The process should be able to absorb complexity but still operate with simplicity and clarity in order to be effective.

Unlike during the Renaissance, we live in a hyperspecialized society. We tend to confront challenges using specialized lenses and a narrow point of view. Over the past few centuries, the funnel of our education system and our approaches to problem-solving have narrowed to a needle-sized point. We are encouraged to have a laser focus in our expertise rather than study broadly. Thus, people who possess great expertise in very specific areas but a limited breadth of experience frequently grapple with complex challenges they are only partly suited to tackle.

Of course, specialization is important. You want a brain surgeon performing brain surgery. You want an engineer designing your bridge. However, some challenges call for broader knowledge. To find a cure for Parkinson's disease, you need not only neurologists, but also gastroenterologists, pulmonologists, kinetic movement specialists, and maybe a brain surgeon. You might also add stem cell researchers, big-data analysts, geneticists, and psychiatrists.

If you're building a smart city and an ecosystem around a new transportation system, you not only want engineers, but policy makers, sociologists, and other academics, as well as the public, employers, employees, vehicle manufacturers, and transportation companies. At the core, what you need for solving complex problems is creative thinking to spur that vision forward—a vision that can be checked in real time by subject-matter experts.

Too often, we default to one specialization at a time when more and more problem sets are interconnected and require both a right-brained and a left-brained approach—tapping into both creative and logical networks, whether that be our own neural network or the networks of those we know.

HOLISTIC THINKING TODAY

If you're like me, you're probably not knowledgeable about *everything*. I sometimes like to think I am, but my wife and kids assure me otherwise. So few people in the history of written society have been true innovators in all fields, their mastery equally permeating the arts and sciences, but true brilliance stems from this convergence.

To compensate for our lack of knowledge, we need holistic thinking in the form of what I call *mixed tables*, which I'll cover in the first half of the book where I delve into how to solve problem sets.

Throughout my life, I've found holistic thinking (and, by consequence, mixed tables) to be one of the most effective methods of problem-solving.

This holistic perspective, emboldened through the Renaissance, embraces a diversity of thought so you can navigate challenging waters in a different and more effective way.

Though many leaders feel overwhelmed these days, I contend that solution sets are not beyond our reach, even for the most complex problems. I'm not suggesting that all problems are solvable—they're not. We can't always find answers to ambiguous questions, and we won't obtain easy answers to the most difficult questions of our time just because we put together a mixed table.

With this in mind, I like to say there are no universal truths other than that there are no universal truths. Ask a physicist about the origins of black holes. If you put sixteen of them in a room, you might get sixteen different answers. That differentiation of opinion is where true gold lies. With a holistic perspective brought about by assembling a variety of people, you have an exponentially better chance of finding a way to overcome any challenge.

I am reminded of a friend who worked for DARPA (Defensive Advanced Research Projects Agency), which was established in the 1950s in response to the Soviet launch of the man-made satellite Sputnik. DARPA is a unique organization in that it values failure just as much as success. In a certain way, failure is considered success in that the mantra is to seriously push the envelope—to boldly go where no one has gone before. If the various components (program managers) of DARPA are constantly "succeeding," they aren't pushing the envelope far enough.

DARPA has accomplished some incredibly remarkable things. Remember when Al Gore invented the internet? Well, the internet was originally called ARPANET and nobody at the time thought it would serve any useful purpose. DARPA also created or had a significant impact on technologies such as the original version of Siri, the GPS, and touchscreens. All one has to do is look at a smartphone to spot DARPA fingerprints.

My buddy, a former project manager for DARPA who prefers to remain anonymous, was interested in social media networks, which are vastly complex. Social media networks sometimes have an inception point, as in the case of Russian interference with the 2016 presidential election, but often they don't. Sometimes they are simply organic, as in the case of the Arab Spring. My colleague was interested in understanding the ways in which social media networks connect, operate, and influence, as there are now huge national-security applications related to their predictive and postscriptive abilities.

He came up with a theory that cancers and social networks operate in the same way. This was not to say that social networks are negative in and of themselves, only that the informational flow may be similar. This inspired him to think about all the scientific databases around the world—diverse pockets of information in disparate locations across the globe. What if these databases could all be tapped into through open-source capabilities to understand what solutions might already exist?

Consider cures for cancer. If the databases weren't communicating with one another, they wouldn't be discovered. In a similar way, information not seen on a social network could contain key pieces of information vital to national security. This realization prompted him to create a program to look at understanding and coming up with a breakthrough for cancer—using one model to look at another and, at the same time, taking a swing at solving one of the great medical mysteries of our lives.

How great is that?

If you can tap into pockets of information and bring them together, you can find connections that lead to solutions you might never have thought of otherwise. This is the essential idea behind a mixed table: thinking holistically.

However, a conceptual solution is merely an answer, not a solution. It has to become real, and making answers real requires a campaign mindset to bring them to life.

YOUR LIFE IS A CAMPAIGN

Humans have been running campaigns since the dawn of consciousness.

Get food. Find shelter. Create tribes for protection. Even as civilizations developed, people acted in accordance with societal expectations.

But in Renaissance England, where the movement truly ignited during King Henry VIII's reign, the Renaissance took on a somewhat different form than Italy's holistic thinking: humanism. To put it simply, people began to think and act for themselves in an unprecedented manner. They began running individual life campaigns, which I'll explore more in the second part of the book, as it revolves around execution and implementing strategies to solve your problem.

A campaign is simply an organized course of action to achieve a particular objective. It has six distinct elements that provide you, the campaign manager, a structured way to accomplish your goals. It's a chassis. It always has the same frame. What you do is change what's on the outside and inside, just like you do when designing cars.

Let's break the chassis down step by step.

- First, intentionally identify your desired outcome.
- Second, understand the context in which you are operating.
- Third, map out the individuals, groups, and organizations you need to navigate on your way to success.
- Fourth, create and articulate a strategy for getting from start to finish.
- Fifth, develop and understand the tactics that move you along.
- Sixth, execute.

That's it. That's a campaign.

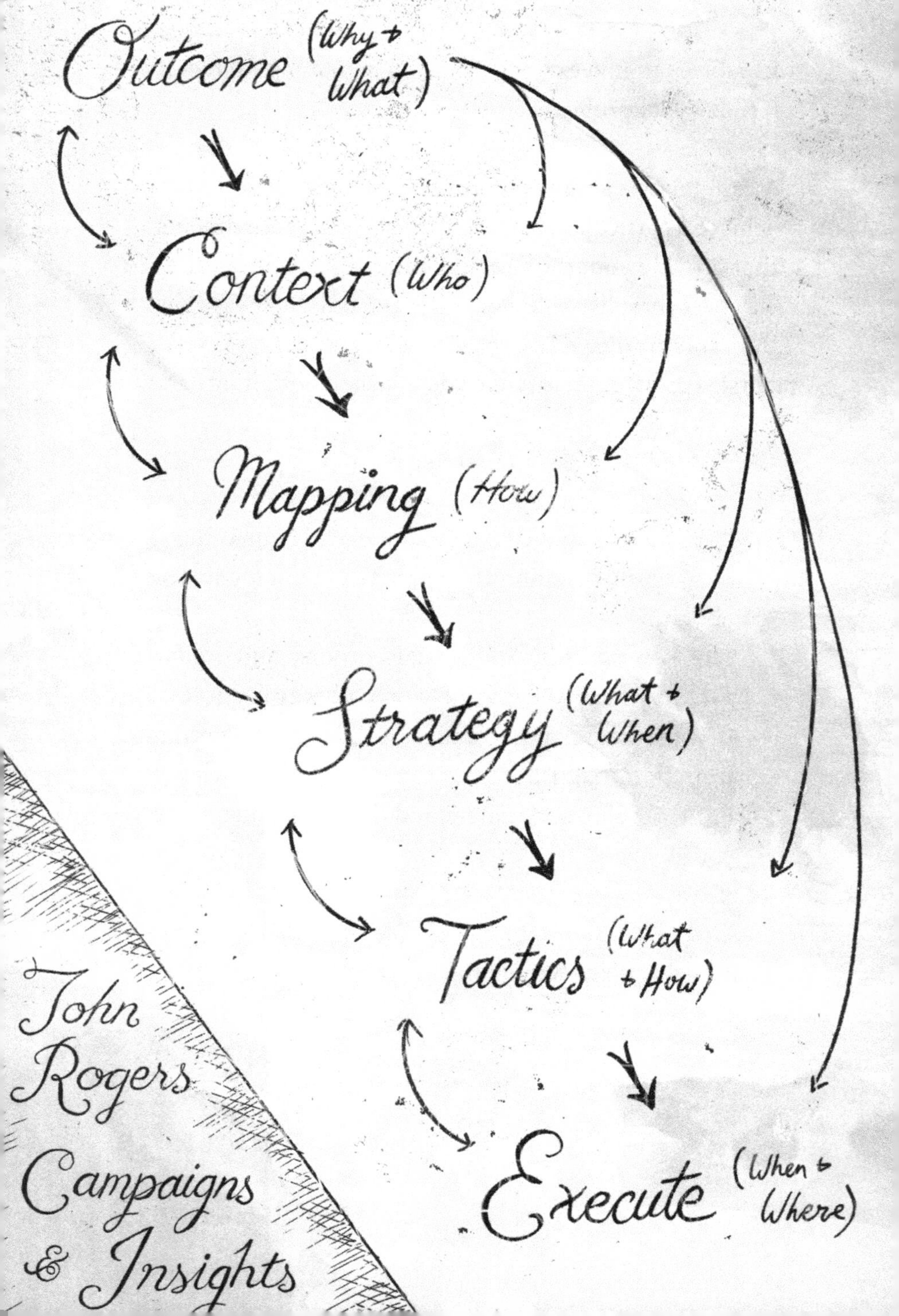

Outcome (Why & What)

Context (Who)

Mapping (How)

Strategy (What & When)

Tactics (What & How)

Execute (When & Where)

John Rogers

Campaigns

& Insights

Over the course of your life, you will run thousands, if not millions, of campaigns. When you work hard to get your kid into a prestigious private school? That's a campaign. When you attempt to close a sales deal, using every sales tactic in the book, that's also a campaign. How about losing ten pounds?

The list is endless. Campaigning is how you get things done. It works for military leaders as well as it does for politicians, marketers, corporate trainers, schoolteachers, and you and me in our daily lives.

Running campaigns is not unlike *The Matrix*. Here's the red pill or the blue pill.

You can choose to do one of two things: keep your eyes closed and continue to operate the way you've been operating, without understanding structure, or open your eyes and recognize that everything you're doing is a campaign, whether you call it one or not.

That's the difference. The choice is yours.

Do you want to just wing it, or do you want to create a structure to achieve your goal more effectively? And are you using all of the tools at your disposal to achieve your objectives?

CUTTING THROUGH THE CLUTTER

In this book, I want to help you develop new approaches to finding answers by thinking holistically. Then, I want to help you effectively implement them.

The world moves really frickin' fast, and the competing priorities fighting for your time are more pervasive than ever. It can feel like it's hard to get *anything* right, much less *everything* right.

That's why so many leaders of the past century have tried to minimize the number of decisions they need to make every day. Think of Steve Jobs wearing the same "uniform" on a daily basis.

These methodologies are intended to provide a more effective way to cut through the clutter, quiet the noise, and achieve your objectives.

You can have holistic thinking without running a campaign, or you can run a campaign without holistic thinking backing it up. The power is when you combine them.

PART ONE

THE ESSENTIAL NATURE OF MIXED-TABLE THINKING

The Need for Holistic, Creative Thought

CHAPTER 1

THE NEED FOR HOLISTIC, CREATIVE THOUGHT

The future is coming, to a life near you.

My parents were a wonderful mix of left brain and right brain.

My father, Buck, was an insurance-company executive whose parents divorced in the 1920s, long before divorce was normalized. He grew up as a Depression-era child doing odd jobs in Kentucky, Indiana, and Chicago to survive. When World War II hit, he had a friend memorize the eye chart so he could enlist, despite being blind in one eye. To him, it was logical: America was attacked, so he should defend it. Later, he was one of the few World War II veterans in our community to speak out against the

Vietnam War. Again, the decision was a logical one. He hated war and didn't believe, in that instance, we should be fighting. He always pushed me to consider problems logically, rather than simply conform to what others in my perceived "group" thought. To this day, I try to honor this way of thinking.

Conversely, my mother, Margaret, was a creative soul with a variety of eclectic pursuits. For twenty-three years, she sang with the Chicago Symphony Chorus under choir director Margaret Hillis and symphony director Georg Solti. At the end of her time, she was the longest serving member of the choir, every member of which had to audition annually to maintain their positions.

She also helped write a dictionary on Hittite (an ancient hieroglyphic language) at the University of Chicago and collected modern art, antiques, and gorgeous Oriental rugs. From classical music to painting, needlepoint, and playwriting, she enjoyed many different forms of art. One such passion was literature and in particular, for reasons I never quite understood, James Joyce.

Her fondness for Joyce went beyond merely reading his modernist, avant-garde novels. She worked with a rock composer named Sigmund Snopek III to create a musical performance based on the ten multilingual portmanteau words of Joyce's *Finnegans Wake*.

She even collaborated with Joycean scholars Gareth and Janet Dunleavy at the University of Wisconsin–Milwaukee. For decades, they, along with scholars internationally, had worked to understand the riddle buried in the strange structure of Joyce's novel *Ulysses*. If you've never read it, *Ulysses* is a novel of eighteen chapters, representing the hours from 8:00 a.m. to 12:00 a.m., and is loosely modeled after the Homeric epic poem *The Odyssey*.

As it turned out, the academics' inability to solve Joyce's riddle had nothing to do with a lack of skill, intelligence, or ability. They just needed a holistic perspective on the problem.

I have to be honest. James Joyce is one of my least favorite authors. For me, reading him is a bit like watching paint dry. However, he is broadly credited as one of the most important avant-garde writers of the early twentieth century. Joyce was a novelist and poet, and, coincidentally, a singer. In truth, if he hadn't made it as a writer, he might have made a career in music.[1] Apparently, he had a wonderful voice and, being Irish, music was a huge part of his cultural heritage.

Through his love of music, Joyce buried a riddle in the structure of the book, which became the essential ele-

---

1   Gerald Gold, "MUSIC; The Many Sounds of Joyce," *New York Times*, January, 31, 1988, www.nytimes.com/1988/01/31/arts/music-the-many-sounds-of-joyce.html.

ment that scholars struggled to understand—until, serendipitous though it might seem, my mother figured it out.

Like Joyce, my mother came from a musical background, so when she analyzed the novel, she noticed something that nonmusical scholars simply couldn't see: *Ulysses* is structured as a fugue, a compositional technique in music in which short musical themes are introduced early in a composition and come up repeatedly at later points throughout. Given her life's dedication to music, my mother was well acquainted with the pattern, and through this intersection of thought, she observed that fragments of text introduced early in *Ulysses* are interwoven through subsequent sections.

It wasn't a failure on the part of Joycean scholars for not realizing this; they simply lacked the necessary outside expertise. By bringing my mother to the table, who was able to apply her musical knowledge to the problem, they found an answer that had eluded scholars for years.

CREATIVE PROBLEM-SOLVING IN A COMBAT ZONE

It's this type of holistic thinking upon which this book hinges. Believe it or not, it's also this type of holistic thinking that directly relates to detecting IED attacks.

Hear me out.

You might remember the frequent news reports about IED attacks during the Iraq and Afghanistan Wars. Maybe it even affected someone you know. Never before had improvised explosives been used with such lethal effect, and it was a source of extreme frustration for military planners. Adding to the problem, the enemy used videos of the attacks as propaganda. One of the biggest challenges for the US military in finding a solution was trying to predict where the enemy would place the IEDs. Many brilliant military minds worked on the problem without much progress.

Ultimately, one of the key insights came from a surprising source—Hollywood filmmakers.

Similar to my mother, someone looking at a challenge from an entirely different perspective uncovered a solution to a pressing challenge. I'm going to talk more deeply about this later in the book, but for now, let me describe an interesting dynamic.

My company, RL Leaders, built an IED simulation system called the Improvised Explosive Device Battle Drill (IEDBD). It was incredible and brought technology usually reserved for flight simulators to soldiers on the ground.

Among other things, we had to examine the placement of IEDs. We turned to a variety of professionals in the national security and entertainment communities, and I'm reminded of a story from a gifted director named Randal Kleiser. Randal was the director of *Grease* (1978) and *Blue Lagoon* (1980), as well as the director of the IED Battle Drill. Though we already knew IEDs were being placed for propaganda, he realized that *how* they were placed optimized the best camera angles. Getting "the shot" was really important for those laying the IEDs.

It was a brilliant aha moment that not only impacted how we went about building the IEDBD but, perhaps more importantly, played a significant role in helping our troops identify where and how the devices were placed, all with the goal of saving lives. Although the IEDBD never fully lived up to its potential for reasons I'll describe later in this book, it's something that everyone who was involved takes enormous pride in to this day.

OVERCOMING GROUPTHINK

Randal's discovery in the IED Battle Drill massively changed our entire approach, in just one of many examples evidencing the importance of holistic thinking. No matter what issues you face in your personal or professional life, new perspectives uncovered by holistic thinking will reap enormous benefits.

In your own organization, your team is almost certainly comprised of highly intelligent, capable people. The fact that some challenges appear to be beyond their abilities is no reflection on their excellence. They may simply lack a wide-enough range of perspectives. On the surface, it makes sense to select team members from the same industry. After all, if you want to tackle an accounting problem, you bring in skilled accountants, right? If you want to reroute downtown streets, you bring in civil engineers.

That's the usual approach, but when every member of a team has relatively homogenous experiences and possesses the same general expertise, you run the risk of falling into groupthink, the very opposite of what the Renaissance represented, and the opposite of what we need today. A depth of knowledge is important, but it's no substitute for a *breadth* of knowledge.

Even first-tier consulting companies fall into this trap. Take McKinsey & Company. Many consider them brilliant—and they may be. However, they also recruit the same people from the same universities over and over again, which yields teams burdened by the same perspectives.

Over time, a homogenous team becomes highly proficient in the tactics that have always worked for them, so leaders instinctively assume those same tactics will continue to work in the future. Those tactics might even work 80 percent of the time, which can reinforce a leader's confidence. However, it's the 20 percent of the time that can unexpectedly cause calamity. When that happens, teams often feel mounting panic as their usual way of solving problems suddenly stops working. In turn, leaders become frustrated with their team.

"Come on, folks. Why can't we figure this out? Let's get on the ball and fix the problem!"

Homogenous thinking is often characterized as "group-think," which, unfortunately, has widespread effects regardless of industry. The term "groupthink" was first used in the 1950s to describe a phenomenon of "rationalized conformity" in which the desire to seek concurrence on an idea overrides any attempt at considering alternative courses of action.

Yale psychologist Irving Janis famously used this term to describe the chain of events that led to the disastrous Bay of Pigs invasion in 1961. President Kennedy had made it clear to his subordinates that he wanted to overthrow Cuban dictator Fidel Castro, and the intensity of his viewpoint led, according to Janis, to a "deterioration of mental efficiency, reality testing, and moral judgment" throughout his cabinet.[2] Rather than present, discuss, or debate other options, his subordinates felt such a need to conform that they only reinforced Kennedy's thinking, which, in turn, caused him to make one of the worst decisions of his presidency.

To Kennedy's credit, he learned from the mistake and subsequently restructured his decision-making process. To defend against the tendency toward groupthink, he created an environment of freewheeling discussions, breaking his team into subgroups, each of which considered alternative ideas, and even occasionally met without Kennedy present. Still, not every administration that has succeeded Kennedy has learned from his example. We probably don't need to name names.

In the private sector, most organizations concentrate on meeting numbers: revenue and expenses, sales, units, KPIs, quarterly results, P&L, and PTI or EBITDA goals. They have the metrics, the tactics, and the same old strategy, and they push for those big numbers every quarter. What they lack is a methodology for devising fresh approaches, so when a new or unexpected challenge comes along, they are thrown for a loop. What they need to do is both at the same time. Of course, they need to operate the business and meet their numbers, but they

---

2   Ben Dattner, PhD, "Preventing 'Groupthink,'" *Psychology Today*, April 20, 2011, https://www.psychologytoday.com/us/blog/credit-and-blame-work/201104/preventing-groupthink.

also need to look far enough into the future to know how to adapt, survive, and thrive.

Kodak serves as a perfect example. A stellar company that thrived for decades, Kodak was an American *institution*—a powerhouse of the photographic industry. More than that, Kodak's team was comprised of cutting-edge innovators who made huge transitions over the course of their history. Founded by George Eastman and Henry Strong in the nineteenth century, their tagline, *a Kodak moment*, became part of the national lexicon. As an amateur photographer, it was certainly a staple in my life for decades.

Initially, Eastman invented a machine that coated glass photographic plates with a gelatin emulsion, which became his primary product. In fact, the original name of the company was the Eastman Film and Dry Plate Company, and his technological innovation made photography more affordable. Just take a second to imagine how affordable photography changed society. Until Eastman, capturing life's moments belonged to the elite, and today we live in a camera-ready, snap-happy culture. It was truly groundbreaking.

Later, when dry plates became old tech, they innovated and evolved, switching their focus to black-and-white film. Eventually, they abandoned their profitable black-

and-white film business and went to color. For years, they changed with the times, remaining central to the photography industry.

Until the twenty-first century.

In the 1990s, they spent $500 million to develop the Advantix system, a precursor to the first digital camera. They even developed the first one-megabyte digital camera, but the company leaders ultimately made a fateful decision: they chose to define themselves first and foremost as a film company. Though they had a study that warned them that the digital age would arrive within ten years, they were now wedded to making chemical film and photographic paper, which would become a thing of the past. They believed they could ride it out. Rigidity of thought had taken hold, so they resisted the call to change.

When the digital age arrived, they were still focusing on chemicals and paper, and it ultimately led to the demise of one of the most iconic brands in American history. Generations would have found it unimaginable that the company could collapse into obscurity, but they did.

My contention is the leadership at Kodak didn't have a broad enough range of perspectives to predict that photographic film's days were numbered. While company meetings might have involved a lot of hand wringing and raised voices, Kodak executives failed to adapt to the digital age and paid a heavy price—a fate shared by many notable organizations of the recent past.

IMAGINATION SPECIALISTS

I've often wondered how to combat rigidity of thought, and I've come to believe that the most important characteristic of a leader is to listen. It's too easy to fall into a pattern of behavior in which decision-making becomes a mere muscle response—doing what you've always done because that's what you've always done. If we don't listen, how can we perceive and prepare for incoming disruptions, ideally ahead of time?

In that sense, holistic thinking is an insurance policy for the future, and I've found tapping into the creative-arts community particularly effective. It's like the *secret sauce* of holistic thinking.

Let's rewind about six hundred years to make sense of this.

The flourishing of artistry during the Renaissance, a time of innovation and forward thinking, wasn't by happenstance. According to Britannica, "It was in art that the spirit of the Renaissance achieved its sharpest formulation."[3] The great artists of the time didn't simply paint or sculpt. They analyzed perspective, anatomy, and balance, turning art into a science, thereby revolutionizing how people perceived the world. With their art, they captured truth in a way Europe had thus far never seen, altering the lives of thousands.

Consider Michelangelo's Sistine Chapel.

Though it was originally a celestial scene, Pope Julius II had the foresight and ingenuity to imagine something far grander. He hired Michelangelo to paint a series of religious frescoes, and (albeit begrudgingly) the sculptor accepted and created a masterpiece that nearly tricks the mind into believing a third dimension has manifested through his brushstrokes, so realistic were his images, entirely unlike the flat paintings of the Middle Ages.

As philosophers looked to the Ancient Greek and Roman civilizations for inspiration, humanism captured Renaissance society. Rather than ignore the context of his time, Michelangelo reconciled these burgeoning humanist beliefs with Catholic views, placing Ancient Greek sibyls alongside characters from the Bible's book of Genesis.

Conversely, in England, the first permanent theater in the

---

3   The Editors of Encyclopaedia Britannica, "Renaissance Art," *ENCYCLOPÆDIA BRITANNICA,* accessed September 18, 2018, https://www.britannica.com/art/Renaissance-art.

country was erected in 1576, ushering in the Renaissance for the less affluent. Famously, groundlings would gather on the floor of the Globe Theatre to watch performances, mainly those penned by William Shakespeare, who also relied heavily upon Greek and Roman mythology in his plays. People were exposed to different perspectives through the power of art, just as different perspectives helped these artistic geniuses to create more art. The more people who were able to partake in this societal holistic thinking, the more cultures across Europe began to fundamentally shift.

Creativity breeds artistry, artistry breeds creativity, and both help shape and create reality. With such an abundance of artistic visions in the Renaissance, it's no wonder society advanced at a rate it hadn't witnessed in centuries.

There's a reason people continue to revel in the art born from that time period, and it's not simply because their creations were "pretty." They encapsulated the brilliance and holistic thinking of the time, which is exactly what the creative-arts community can still provide today.

Today, we can't call da Vinci, Michelangelo, or Shakespeare to help us, though I'm sure the conversations would be fascinating if we could. But we do have valuable creatives to help inspire holistic thinking, whether that means Hollywood filmmakers, a local theater director, or a celebrated local artist.

When I first started involving the Hollywood creative-arts community in national security, critics wondered what Hollywood could possibly contribute to such discussions. It sounds a little crazy, doesn't it? However, a typical Hollywood writer does more research on a wider variety of topics than anyone can possibly imagine. Writers must be resourceful and quick-thinking, all while dealing with tight deadlines. When working on a TV series, they have to pound out multiple drafts of a script every week, so they operate under constant pressure.

These people are gifted, experienced, and trained imagination mavens accustomed to working within a time budget. Their unique experiences make them ideal for tackling unusual challenges with surprising, fresh ideas.

Whether you're listening to people in creative fields or to people in worlds vastly different from your own, remaining attentive to holistic thinking is a key element of leadership. In my belief, it's one of the last defenses we can employ to prevent our companies from crumbling in changing times.

HOW I LEARNED THIS THOUGHT PROCESS

We all have mentors, and mine was instrumental in helping me develop this predilection toward holistic thinking. That mentor was former secretary of defense Les Aspin.

Early in my career, I worked for Congressman Les Aspin as his ombudsman (district director). A representative from southeastern Wisconsin, and a moderate Democrat, he represented a district that encompasses the cities of Elkhorn, Janesville, Kenosha, Racine, Lake Geneva, and Beloit. It's the seat that was later occupied by Speaker of the House Paul Ryan. Aspin was a brilliant man, with an undergraduate degree from Yale, a master's from Oxford, and a PhD from MIT.

Les remains one of the smartest people I've ever known, filled with passion and a commitment to his country that ultimately became his undoing. At the same time, he was notoriously tough and demanding.

We had staff meetings on Sunday mornings at a beat-up cottage on Lake Beulah in East Troy, Wisconsin, and I remember one of those meetings with great clarity. I ran a campaign to clean Delavan Lake in Wisconsin (my family has had a long history on that lake). Back in the 1980s, the lake was full of algae. In order to clean it, we had to restore the national Clean Lakes Program, which had been eliminated by President Ronald Reagan. I was put in charge of designing the campaign, strategy, and tactics for getting this done.

We succeeded. It was a big deal; I was riding high and feeling pretty cocky about it. Aspin brought me back down to earth. While we were sitting in his backyard, he started grilling me.

"So, John, tell me how they're going to clean up the lake."

"Well, they are going to drain it, do a fish kill, seal the bottom of the lake, and build some peninsulas."

"How are they going to drain the lake?" he repeated.

"I'm not really sure."

"Okay, find out. Will it impact any wells?"

"Don't know, boss."

"Find out. How long will the lake be drained? What's the time frame and process for the lake to rise again?"

"I really don't know."

"John, you need to know this stuff. I want to know exactly how they're going to drain it. What are the water levels going to be for every household in the district? Who's in charge of it? What's the time frame?"

"Okay, I'll find out."

"What about the fish kill? How are they going to do it? Why are they doing it? Are they going to restock it? With what kind of fish? When?"

I didn't have the answers because, quite frankly, I didn't know. I hadn't probed deeply into the methodology of cleaning up Delavan Lake. All I had was a basic, vague sense of what needed to be done. Understandably, Aspin wasn't okay with this.

"What about the peninsulas? How does that impact the lake? What are the long-term consequences?"

He prodded me for every detail of the cleanup operation, most of which I couldn't provide.

Afterward, his chief of staff and my great colleague, Ted Bornstein, said to me, "Now you know what it's like to be a hostile witness in front of the chairman of the House Armed Services Committee. That's exactly how it feels."

I was really upset. I'd just achieved a huge win. We'd restored the Clean Lakes Program, and Les Aspin was kicking my ass. I'd been working for him for a while, but suddenly the honeymoon was over.

Finally, seeing that I was pissed, Les looked at me and said, "Hey, John, don't get mad. I was just curious."

That single statement has inspired me and defined the rest of my life.

I was just curious.

Since then, I've done everything I can to be prepared and never get caught flat-footed again. If you own something, own it. From then on, I owned the cleanup of Delevan Lake, and you can be damn sure that at the next staff meeting, I had all the answers. I wasn't going to repeat that performance ever again.

I also constantly drive everyone crazy by asking questions. More importantly, I realize the value and importance of curiosity. What I learned from Les is that curiosity allows us to come up with better answers. With curiosity, we run better campaigns. We *think* more, and the difference that makes is astounding. It might sound inconsequential, but I've found it to be a core tenet of my life and a defining feature of humanity that will differentiate us from artificial intelligence (AI) machines in years to come.

Aspin helped shape more than my career. He shaped my way of thinking—but that's not to minimize his toughness. Later, I came down with Legionnaires' disease while traveling with him to Texas because a helicopter kicked up some dust that got into my lungs. I was running a fever of 104, flat on my back at home, when Ted, his chief of staff, called me.

"You have to get to the staff meeting."

Bear in mind, I lived about an hour and a half from Lake Geneva, where the meeting took place.

"I can't make it," I said. "I'm sick."

"You have to be there. Les is insisting that you make a presentation. The meeting is all about what you're doing. 'Do you want to work for me or not?' will be his attitude. It's up to you. Whatever you want."

I drove to the staff meeting with a 104-degree fever and made my presentation. I got through it, left immediately afterward, and drove straight home. I hated it at the time, but it taught me levels of resiliency and toughness that have served me well throughout my career.

WAKE UP! THE FUTURE IS COMING!

My story about learning toughness reflects my belief that you must develop rhino skin. While Bette Davis may be right, "Growing old ain't for sissies," the same can be said for understanding the future, disruptions, shaping the world, and unknown unknowns.[4]

In his book *The Four*, Scott Galloway discusses the major disruptions caused by Amazon, Google, Facebook, and Apple. Amazon has single-handedly changed retail space. Google is the closest thing to God that many people will ever know (ask Google a question, and receive an answer from on high). Facebook has more users than there are people in China, and Apple has redefined technology as a luxury, making tech cool that had formerly been considered geeky.

As computer power increases, with machine learning and quantum computing on the horizon, the pace of disruption will only continue to rise. Five years ago, AI was little more than sophisticated statistical modeling, but tomorrow it may be able to analyze, synthesize, and use data in ways humans have never conceptualized. With this confluence of factors staring leaders in the face, we need tools that are both quantitative (able to process massive

---

4   Roz Warren, *Women's Lip: Outrageous, Irreverent and Just Plain Hilarious Quotes* (Naperville, IL: Sourcebooks, 2006), 179.

amounts of data) and qualitative (able to analyze that data from the perspective of human experience).

Hopefully, the framework this book provides will empower organizations to approach problem-solving in a new, more effective way. As a result, perhaps leaders will embrace causing disruption rather than being disrupted. Maybe a leader will say, "I need to get that scientist I met on the airplane last week to meet with this attorney who has argued in front of the Supreme Court, so we can consider our current challenges from fresh perspectives." It's that kind of thinking that's going to make a difference as society advances.

My call to arms is simple. Wake up! The future is coming!

DO YOU NEED A HOLISTIC PERSPECTIVE?

Are you thinking about the unknown unknowns in your industry?

Do you have a long-standing, stubborn problem you're trying to solve?

Is it a recalcitrant problem?

Is it merely a technical problem?

Is the problem multifaceted?

Will the challenge be worthwhile?

Is it a big enough problem to need multiple perspectives?

Do you have the right team looking into the problem? If not, what other perspectives and insights could be useful?

Remember, it's one thing to need your furnace repaired; it's another thing to design what the future of furnaces looks like using new forms of energy—a technical yet visionary solution that may require more than a technical perspective.

A Mixed Table

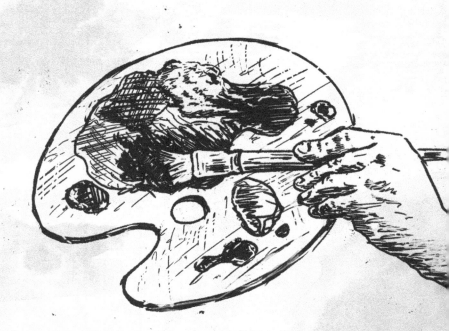

CHAPTER 2

MIXED TABLES AND HOW THEY ADVANCE SOCIETY

The minds of many outweigh the minds of a few.

Holistic thinking is essential, but it requires structure. Therein lies the brilliance of something called the *mixed table*, a collaboration between people who wouldn't ordinarily have the opportunity to convene in a meaningful way, such as experts from diverse fields. Together, they inspire creative, holistic thinking, thereby providing leaders with a smarter, more thoughtful approach to problem-solving.

Aspin taught me the process. My colleagues Erik Oksala, Brian Layer, and Richard Lindheim helped me define and improve it. However, the foundation is a methodology humans have relied upon for centuries.

MEDICI AND THE MANHATTAN PROJECT

Though they didn't use the term "mixed table," wise people have long grasped the importance of bringing diverse perspectives together to tackle society's toughest challenges.

Take the House of Medici, a banking family that dominated the political sphere in the Republic of Florence from the fifteenth century to the eighteenth century. As owners and operators of the largest bank in Europe, their wealth catapulted them into politics, granting them power and influence. At the time of their ascension, the plague had decimated much of Europe, leaving many affluent families with a yearning to make their mark upon the world, through which the Medicis' greatest accomplishment was born.

In *The Medici Effect*, Frans Johansson describes the Medicis' desire for a community that was *different*—that stood apart because of its art, humanism, and beauty. In a perhaps unparalleled restructuring of culture the Western world has not witnessed since, the Medicis amassed painters, architects, stonemasons, financial experts, poets, and playwrights. This diverse assemblage collaborated and actualized a new and compelling vision for the city that many historians credit for ushering in the Renaissance.

At a time when artists depended upon commissions from wealthy supporters, the Medicis proved especially generous. A number of famous Renaissance artists, including Michelangelo, Botticelli, and Leonardo da Vinci, were beneficiaries of the Medici family, and a significant proportion of the gorgeous architecture in Florence was funded by the family and created by their community of skilled artisans.[5]

The result of their work can be enjoyed to this day, six hundred years after they began the transformation. Florence is one of the most beautiful and fascinating cities in the world, serving as an extraordinary example of how mixed tables can have a lasting impact on society.

Though da Vinci is often perceived as the quintessential Renaissance man, his rival Michelangelo was a brilliant polymath in his own right. Historical tales indicate that he wasn't the most pleasant dinner companion, but as a philosopher, architect, painter, and sculptor, he had an exquisite mind and created breathtaking art. One such piece is *David*, a product of his professional relationship with the Medici family.

A few years ago, I had the privilege of seeing it in Florence,

5   Mike Colagrossi, "The Rise and Fall of the Medici Family: How They Created and Lost Their Banking Empire," *Big Think, Big Think*, July 8, 2018, bigthink.com/mike-colagrossi/how-the-medici-family-created-and-lost-their-banking-empire.

and even then, I knew its impact would last long after our flight home, while I was still stuffed from too much pasta.

The docent who brought my family and me into the gallery had us do something rather unusual. First, she instructed us to look at *David* from forty yards away.

"Notice the expression on his face," she said. "Remember that look."

Then, we closed the gap and stood at the base of the statue. "Look at his expression now. Has it changed?"

Surprisingly, it had. The emotions etched into his face struck a different chord from this angle.

Next, the docent had us walk around the statue, and as we continued to study his expression and disposition, we witnessed a range of emotions, depending on where we stood. From one angle, he seemed determined. From another, angry. Then, fearful. From yet another, lustful. Finally, he appeared resolved. I found it haunting yet difficult to describe, for it wasn't simply a shift in posture or trick of the light creating an illusion. The very soul in his eyes altered with each movement, as if Michelangelo had truly brought this man to life.

Every perspective brought us another interpretation of the object, not unlike the experience of the mixed table.

View a bit of this for yourself in the series of photos I shot, which I've provided below. However, if you ever get the chance to see it in person, do it.

A highly different example is the Manhattan Project, which allowed for a swifter end to World War II but propelled the world into the atomic age. From 1942 until 1946, the Manhattan Project brought diverse forces to bear in the creation of the atomic bomb, including mathematicians, physicists, chemists, engineers, military leaders, policymakers, and thought leaders. Characterized a different way, the Manhattan Project was an extraordinarily sophisticated mixed table. Led by the United States, with help from Canada and the United Kingdom, it was a gargantuan effort—and an arms race.

It doesn't take watching the terrific series *Man in the High Castle* to imagine a world in which Nazi Germany developed the atomic bomb first. The scale of devastation the Nazi regime would have wrought with atomic weapons is terrifying to contemplate. Fortunately, by creating a mixed table that included some of the most intelligent people in the world from a wide range of fields, the United States won the race and brought an end to the war.

Whether considering marble facades in Florence or the Second World War's decimated cities, mixed tables shape society, bring about massive shifts in human history, and determine the fates of peoples and nations.

The power of holistic thinking gave rise to the Renaissance period *and* brought an end to World War II. It can also help us deal with our personal and professional challenges today, no matter how big, complex, or intractable.

POLYMATHS NEED MIXED TABLES, TOO

In past years, people on both sides of the political spectrum have articulated the need for divergent thinking.

Hillary Clinton said, "It takes a village," and President George H. W. Bush said, "A thousand points of light," and they're both absolutely right.

It does take a village.

It does take a thousand points of light.

Why? Because few of us are true polymaths, as typified by the Renaissance man or woman. With origins in the 1400s, the term *Renaissance man* refers to those who excel at a great many pursuits. In my opinion, the ultimate example of a polymath was Leonardo da Vinci, a brilliant inventor and genius in both the arts and sciences.

There are also people in my own life who have seeds of this brilliance. My friend Mike Wiener is a distinguished psychiatrist and brain scientist, as well as a winemaker, jazz musician, and athlete. He wakes up and swims in the San Francisco Bay every morning *sans* wetsuit. He's particularly passionate about bringing a more open-source approach to science, because he's convinced it will lead to faster and better cures for many diseases. Because of his efforts, Mike has greatly advanced research into Alzheimer's and Parkinson's.

As a retired army colonel who jumps out of airplanes in the middle of the night, as well as a brilliant writer, philosopher, and fashion guru, my great friend Michael Landrum also stands out as a Renaissance man. So does David Semmel, who started a software company in his garage and sold it, and then went on to start a venture fund, a hedge fund, and a beer company, all while gardening, biking, skiing, and playing guitar. Kelly Fitzsimmons (speaker, CEO, technologist, futurist, advocate, coach) had a zest for the new and intellectually pure. Paul Grunau (CEO, athlete, mentor of many) is another Renaissance person due to his deep curiosity, as is Désirée van Gorp—lawyer, business professor, public relations professional, antique and art collector, and caregiver.

Then there are those we read about like Queen Margrethe of Denmark, Sting, Elon Musk, Mayim Bialik, and W. E. "Ed" Bosarge.

What all of these people have in common is a curiosity and desire to learn more, try more, and advance the world. How great is that?

One might argue that polymaths don't need or use mixed tables. While they may have their own form of brilliance,

I would suggest otherwise. They know how to tap into greater knowledge than their own in pursuit of their curiosities.

Many consider da Vinci the archetype of a polymath, yet he didn't work alone. A notorious note-taker, he recorded his thoughts, questions, and reminders in notebooks, many of which involved lists of people he wanted to seek answers from when stumped. As outlined in Toby Lester's book *Da Vinci's Ghost: Genius, Obsession, and How Leonardo Created the World in His Own Image,* da Vinci would record notes such as, "Ask Maester Antonio how mortars are positioned on bastions by day or night," and "Get the Maester of Arithmetic to show you how to square a triangle." If we all jotted down similar notes to ourselves, how much more expansive would our understanding of the world be?

Given his lasting impression on society, it would be easy to deify people like da Vinci, as if the man was born exceptional, with no need to learn or grow, but that's absurd. His mind was magnificent because of his insatiable curiosity and appetite for knowledge. As far as history's eye can see, he never allowed something as insignificant as pride to prevent him from seeking answers and learning more about the universe.

In discussing this with my daughter, Alex, she made an

interesting point. For centuries, human beings relied on a literal village just to get by. Individuals didn't generally try to accomplish everything on their own. They knew they had a community of skilled people around them, which gave them access to a wide array of expertise.

We've evolved as a society, yet countless studies indicate we've become more isolated. Technology, which is designed to connect us, has also bred isolation, and these days, we expect individuals to encompass an unattainable number of skills and qualities.

I think Alex has hit the nail on the head. In many ways, society is retreating into new, unhealthy forms of tribalism and isolationism. Information assaults our senses, and given today's political acrimony and echo chambers, when people don't know what to believe, they simply believe what aligns with their viewpoints, versus hunting for the most intellectually pure answers.

It still takes a village. It still takes a thousand points of light. It still takes seeking others for their knowledge and wisdom.

Nobody, not even the most gifted polymath, can excel at everything. We need the insights and expertise of others, and reaching this divergent thinking is more important than ever.

We're more driven by AI and data than ever before, but we often lack an organic platform to create human insight into the data. Even with the rise of artificial intelligence, our biggest innovations continue to come from applying creative human thinking to data analysis. What if we could draw upon the expertise of a wide range of people to grapple with our own personal or professional challenges? Well, we can, and more importantly, we *should*. If we bring together those thousand points of light and surround ourselves with a village, we will have the holistic perspective we need to look at problems from multiple angles.

THE CONTEMPORARY MIXED TABLE

While the concept of pulling divergent thinking together is clearly not new, Les Aspin developed a specific methodology around it, which my partners and I refined and now utilize in my company, RL Leaders. A collection of mixed thinkers around a table is now, simply, a *mixed table*.

In the late 1980s, Les Aspin was the chairman of the House Armed Services Committee at a time when Democrats were perceived as soft on defense. Clearly, one of Les's goals was to be in a position of leadership so he could help change this perception and shape defense policy for the future. Under President Bill Clinton, that goal reached its crescendo.

Along with Larry Smith, member services director of the House Armed Services Committee, Aspin devised mixed tables, which, at the time, was a fascinating new program. As described earlier in this chapter, the mixed-tables program assembled a diverse group of people who normally wouldn't have sat at the same table. In this case, he invited Democratic campaign operatives along with independents working in national security and other industries.

Working with Les, I traveled across the country and organized mixed-table dinners in multiple cities. He had three ideal outcomes. First, these meetings were intended to help him create a blueprint for a new defense policy in light of the collapse of the Soviet Union. Second, as chairman of the House Armed Services Committee, he wanted to build a network of relationships across the country, so in that sense, these meetings had a self-serving goal. Third, as stated, Democrats were viewed as soft on defense, which he was committed to changing.

I found the diversity of these meetings fascinating: a local pollster sitting next to a retired army general; a college professor beside the CEO of a defense company. Aspin directed these meetings like a master conductor, laying out his worldview and encouraging the flow of creative ideas.

Given the abrupt end of the Cold War, the United States

was navigating uncharted waters, and foreign policy was up in the air. This presented a vast, open-ended problem, and everyone at the table was invited to share their thoughts on a variety of related topics, including the treatment of returning veterans. Democrats were still experiencing a hangover from the Vietnam War, and when veterans returned, in the worst-case scenario, they were berated and spit at. In the best-case scenario, they were put in the metaphorical closet: "Johnny's finally home. The war was awful, so he did bad things. Let's not talk about it."

Today, no matter the conflict, veterans are treated with respect across the political spectrum. Many people felt that President George W. Bush's invasion of Iraq was a huge mistake. Still, the attitude toward veterans returning from that war did not reflect disagreement with policymakers in the Bush administration. People treated them with honor and respect, including both Vietnam veterans who'd declared, "never again," and politicians who strongly disagreed with the war.

Mixed tables helped make that progress a reality.

Through holistic thinking and mixed tables, Aspin gradually refined an approach that became the blueprint for the Clinton administration's defense policy. The president-elect, impressed by what he saw, nominated

Aspin to become secretary of defense, and the rest is history.

Living this experience up close as a staffer for Les opened my eyes to the power of mixed tables at an early point in my career, which served me well. For instance, in the early 2000s, I became heavily involved in patient advocacy, working with Michael J. Fox and the Parkinson's Action Network. In 2006, the head of the army's medical research division for brain injuries and brilliant physiologist, Colonel Karl Friedl, asked me to help organize a series of mixed tables on a variety of scientific topics. We looked at numerous research "verticals" such as stem cells, neuroimaging, and movement disorders, and we asked the question, "Given unlimited resources, what would it take for a breakthrough to occur as related to Parkinson's?"

The common thread was how surprisingly little crosstalk there frequently is within the scientific community. It proved to me that holistic thinking and mixed tables were much more broadly needed than just within government.

THE COURAGEOUS FIRST STEPS

Mixed tables work in practically all times and places to tackle complex problems, whether dealing with IEDs in

Iraq, turning Florence into a haven for art and humanism, or helping end World War II.

They also provide a construct for discussing really difficult subjects. It's not easy to have completely open and honest conversations about hard topics in the public sphere, but a mixed table creates that environment, though it requires courage and trust from all parties. Ultimately, this will prove to be important in order to solve some of the complex problems associated with sensitive topics, particularly when people are increasingly polarized and issues are increasingly politicized.

If we truly want to advance society, intelligent, insightful people must be able to share their real thoughts without fear of backlash, and a mixed table, done well, can provide that opportunity.

So where does the process begin?

The first step is identifying the best question for what you are trying to achieve. What are you trying to figure out? What is your challenge? And all of the questions surrounding that challenge? This is vital because you use those questions to identify the people you should invite to the mixed table. The second step is to bring together those smart, thoughtful, and insightful people. It takes a bold, confident leader to take that second step.

It takes courage because every organization and its culture are resistant to change. That's how you end up being Kodak.

Once you intellectually understand the value of a mixed table, the next step is making one happen. What you, as a leader, understand is that bringing others along can often be the hard part. Knowing that, of course, is half the battle. The rest is understanding at a deep level how mixed tables work. That's the next section of this book, but remember the first secret: until you've seen the magic happen in front of your very eyes, there will be enormous skepticism.

Mixed Tables
in Action

CHAPTER 3

MIXED TABLES IN ACTION

3 creatives + 3 subject-matter experts + 1 thought leader = a solution

Who thinks about terrorism? Terrorists think about terrorism. The national security community thinks about terrorism. Some parts of academia think about terrorism. The media thinks about terrorism. Those in the private sector with something to lose think about terrorism (or, at least, they should).

But Hollywood and the creative-arts community also think about terrorism.

Authors like Tom Clancy and John le Carré have spent countless hours researching, studying, and defeating terrorism in their stories. Hollywood is filled with prolific writers and other creative types who think and talk about ways to deal with terrorism, concocting hypothetical scenarios and resolutions that play out in best-selling novels, motion pictures, and television shows all the time.

In recent years, the government has begun to utilize this brilliant resource, though it wasn't always so.

THE 9/11 PROJECT

The 9/11 attacks changed us.

I still remember passing the Pentagon while driving down George Washington Parkway in Virginia. I was on the phone with my mother, watching the planes fly in the wrong direction, and told her that I suspected Washington or Chicago would be hit next. By the time I'd traveled the five miles to Old Town, Alexandria, the Pentagon had been hit.

It was a moment in time that subverted much of what we believed about America's defenses, and it united all Americans. Experts hadn't predicted it, and in the aftermath, those same experts scrambled to figure out the right responses.

A couple of key initiatives took place. First, President

Bush convened a meeting of Hollywood studio executives to facilitate different ways of thinking about 9/11. Although this was probably an interesting discussion, it failed in its implementation and never fully came into fruition.

There was a second initiative that proved more valuable. A thoughtful and courageous leader in the army, Mike Andrews, Deputy Assistant Secretary Army RD&E, reached out to my colleague in the creative-arts community, Dick Lindheim, and asked him to convene Hollywood writers, producers, and directors to think about terrorism. Dick is a brilliant guy. Though educated as an engineer, he became a Hollywood executive and rose through the ranks at Paramount/NBC/Universal, ultimately becoming vice president of Universal and vice president of NBC. During his tenure, he was responsible for hits like *Star Trek: The Next Generation*, *MacGyver*, and *Smokey and the Bandit*.

While he was at Universal, Anita Jones, Director of Defense Research and Engineering (DDR&E), asked him a key question, "What can Hollywood do for the Department of Defense?"

Dick knew that people's primordial response to virtually any circumstance is driven by emotion, and who is better at evoking an emotional response than Hollywood?

So naturally, his response was, "Quite a bit."

Ultimately, what began that day led to me hand-delivering a report to senior defense officials and congressional leadership. It was a day I was pretty sure could only go one of three ways. The first was they'd pat me on the head and say, "That's nice, Johnny, but we've thought of all this already." The second was, "This is crazy, Rogers. We're revoking your security clearance forever." The third was what actually occurred. The response was, "Wow, we haven't thought about approaching the problem this way before. This is really interesting."

Parenthetically, three years later, the 9/11 Commission Report was issued. It identified a lack of imagination and creativity as a key shortcoming of the national security community around terrorism, validating Secretary Andrews's and our approach.

Within the national security community, there was widespread amazement at what these "Hollywood types" had come up with. The inclusion of creative people provided a new lens through which the military and national security community could view a complex problem. While bold and visionary leaders grasped the significance of this, most did not. Even so, what began as a mixed table with twenty LA professionals turned into an ongoing program and relationship that in one way, shape, or another continues to this day.

BOLDLY GO WHERE NO ONE HAS GONE BEFORE

It shouldn't be surprising. Writers and filmmakers have often inspired other industries to advance society. Consider the handheld communicators in the original *Star Trek* series. Writers imagined it would be a convenient way for characters on alien planets to communicate with characters aboard a ship, but *Star Trek* communicators provided direct inspiration for the cell phones people use today.

In fact, *Star Trek* has inspired many modern-day gadgets. The phaser "set on stun" became the Taser. *Star Trek*'s universal translator became a Google app that allows users to easily translate a wide variety of languages. Dr. McCoy's tricorder inspired devices like the LOCAD (Lab-on-a-Chip Applications Development), a handheld device that monitors and identifies microbes. Geordi La Forge's visor has also become a reality with the development of bionic eyes. Maybe someday we'll even have transporters, warp drive, and holodecks.

Star Trek also inspired social change with its vision of a multicultural, multiethnic starship crew. Famously, the first interracial kiss ever broadcast on American television happened between Captain Kirk and Lieutenant Uhuru. At a time when the nation was struggling with segregation and racism, caught up in racial tension and violence, the creators behind *Star Trek* envisioned great advances for society. Though we're still struggling to fully realize that vision, we've made much progress, in part because of moments like this.

However, *Star Trek* certainly wasn't the only instigator of change.

Neil Stephenson's 1992 novel *Snow Crash* established his reputation as one of science fiction's most visionary authors, and many of his concepts have manifested in today's world. In the novel, he imagines a dystopian version of America in which the federal government has crumbled in the face of corporate interests. Notably, in the world of *Snow Crash*, there exists a virtual world called the "metaverse," which users can explore through avatars. They can shop at virtual stores, go to online nightclubs, or lounge in their own virtual homes.

This vision became a reality in 2003 when Linden Labs launched their online world, *Second Life*, which bears many similarities to the metaverse.[6] Stephenson also predicted Google Earth. In the novel, one of the main

---

6   "Braving a New World," *The Guardian,* October 24, 2006, https://www.theguardian.com/books/2006/oct/24/fiction.

characters, Hiro, receives a gift of some exotic, hard-to-obtain software. Included in the software suite is a 3-D re-creation of the entire globe, formed by intelligence satellites orbiting the earth. Sound familiar? In the book, this application is simply called "Earth," but it is almost identical to the Google Earth we know and love (or hate) today.

While *Star Trek* had a mostly positive spin on technology, other futuristic stories were much more cautionary. One of my favorite authors, Ray Bradbury, wrote *Fahrenheit 451*, which paid particular attention to the relationship between technology and sensory stimulation. At one point in the story, the author describes the protagonist's wife, Mildred, using what are essentially earbuds, little seashells that produce "an electronic ocean of sound, of music and talk and music and talk coming in, coming in on the shore of her unsleeping mind." With the earbuds, Mildred never has to spend a waking moment away from her beloved media. Today, it only takes glancing at people on a subway, bus, plane, or sidewalk to see how earbuds have become like appendages providing an endless stream of music and podcasts to consume our waking hours.

And then there's Jules Verne, a writer whose legacy lives on in both classrooms and imaginations. In his novel *20,000 Leagues under the Sea*, Verne envisioned a deep-sea submarine that could stay underwater for days at a time long before scientists and engineers brought such a contraption to life.

It sounds simple, but the creative-arts community creates and, in doing so, provides a visionary board that innovators in other fields can study. Who knows what fantastical, seemingly magical concepts featured in today's stories will come to pass for future generations?

I'm still waiting for *Star Wars*-level intergalactic travel.

As previously mentioned, creativity extends far beyond writers hunched over their desks. There are innovators in all fields influencing one another on a grand scale. Take, for example, DARPA, the federal agency that created breakthrough technology for national security that became critical in the development of modern cell phones, inspiring everything from the GPS to Siri. Brilliant entrepreneurs took DARPA's revolutionary ideas and found ways to commercialize them for the public.

Lastly, though an odd example on the surface, consider Viagra, the brand name for Sildenafil, which was created as a heart medicine. As I'm sure you know, that is not where it found commercial success. Scientists using the drug to treat hypertension and heart disease noted a rather peculiar physiological side effect during clinical trials, which led to what is known as "drug repositioning," an evolution of creative thinking made possible by the chemists' open-mindedness and willingness to look outside their immediate area of expertise. Viagra has been a popular pill ever since.

Though occurring on broad societal levels, these are all mixed tables in action, which the Renaissance helped pave the way for, and which I believe we need to foster even more as we move forward in our increasingly complex society.

The Secret Sauce

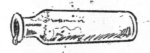

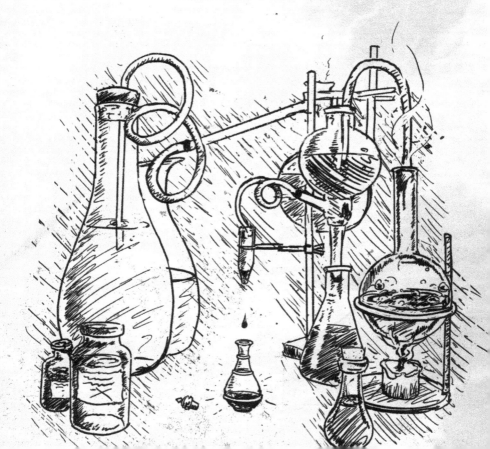

CHAPTER 4

DEEP APPLIED CREATIVITY

There are many paths, young Skywalker. Choose wisely.

At RL Leaders, after years of trial and error, we've developed a much-refined version of Aspin's original mixed-table method, which we call Deep Applied Creativity™.

Once again, it first starts with a question. Address a specific issue or challenge with a clear outcome in mind. That outcome might be multifaceted or a simple desire to validate what you think you know. It could be an aspiration to challenge an assumption, to learn, or to gain a clearer idea of what the future holds. Whatever the case, it always starts with a question. Get as specific as you can, developing a variety of sub-questions to your central question.

Next, with these questions in mind, a panel is molded. Panels should have three types of individuals: creative thinkers, subject-matter experts, and thought leaders. Personally, I hate these labels, but I don't yet have better terms to offer you.

If you think about the panel participants as a concentric circle, the core of Deep Applied Creativity™ are the creative thinkers. (By the way, I can make an argument that virtually anyone is creative. In this context, I'm speaking of people who are paid and making a living from thinking creatively.) I like using Hollywood creatives for this. My partner, Brigadier General Brian Layer (Ret.), has come up with a great description, calling them "paid imaginers working under a time budget." That's important. It's important on the paid imaginers side in that this is what they're paid to do for a living, so they will prompt and stimulate your group in a way that few others can.

The time budget is critical because these people are used to producing creative results in a confined period of time. The Thursday evening deadline for that sitcom isn't going to wait until Friday afternoon for someone to come up with a concept; the show's writers have to produce content by the deadline no matter what. Put slightly differently, they won't partake in a blue-sky exercise that goes on and on, as we've all participated in before.

If you can't access Hollywood, the good news is you can find creativity anywhere. Creativity is like a muscle, and just like an athlete, using that muscle strengthens it. We all have creative potential, but if we don't make the most of it, the muscle atrophies. The creative-arts community is where you find the superstar athletes: those who have tapped into their creative potential and excel at it.

Of course, just because someone is associated with the arts doesn't mean he or she is right for a mixed table. Being able to play a musical instrument isn't enough. It's not just about being creative. You will have to apply a filter to determine which people possess true *creative thinking*. I tend to look for the kind of people who routinely take disparate pieces and assemble them in powerful or thought-provoking ways. They move people, inspire them, disturb them, and take discussions in surprising directions, helping others see a problem and its possible solutions from new and unexpected angles.

Again, Renaissance greats perfectly typify this. William Shakespeare didn't simply write plays. His creativity extended to his manner of thinking: playing with the foundations of language, inventing his own words when he found nothing suitable. To this day, we have him to thank for words such as *champion, birthplace, advertising, hurried, luggage, negotiate, pedant, undress, summit, grovel, secure, dauntless, excitement, dwindle, obsequiously, tran-*

quil, fashionable, and more. In total, he conceived over 1,700 of our common words.[7]

The next ring of the concentric circle is *subject-matter experts* who have a deep understanding of the problem at hand as soon as they walk through the door. Typically, these people come out of your organization and have in-depth knowledge of the issues at hand. That's their strength. Their weakness is that they frequently have their own version of rigidity of thought. Moreover, they may come to the mixed table with heavy skepticism. That's okay, as long as they're open-minded, intellectually adroit, thoughtful, and insightful.

Finally, you need trusted *thought leaders* at your mixed table. These should include diverse people from a variety of backgrounds and levels of success who are insightful and have already accomplished amazing feats. They shouldn't all look like you or each other, as they're there to provide unexpected insight.

With all three of these groups, you have an effective mixed table. Whether or not you make them sign a nondisclosure agreement is up to you, but, remember, you are entrusting yourself to these people. By exposing your

---

7   Amanda Mabillard, "Words Shakespeare Invented," *Shakespeare Online*, accessed September 18, 2018, http://shakespeare-online.com/biography/wordsinvented.html.

problem and limitations, you make yourself vulnerable, so make sure you can trust them.

If you're in need of rapid decision-making in your mixed table, ideas can be grouped together to make sense of the overarching theme. This is referred to as an "associative barrier," and it enables your mixed table to assess a dilemma quickly and efficiently. However, it doesn't come without risks, especially when dealing with complex issues. Making a quick decision about a problem when you lack information simply because you've associated it with something familiar can be counterproductive.

THE SUM IS GREATER THAN THE PARTS

Often, when creating a mixed table, subject-matter experts from relevant fields won't understand why they're surrounded by creatives. You might initially see them with their arms crossed, averting their eyes, with a look on their faces that says, "What am I doing in this room with *these people*?"

By the time the panel is finished, their attitudes will completely transform. Body language changes. People lean forward, animated and enthusiastic, and something magical happens: your subject-matter experts become creatives.

As I've said before, most people have a greater degree

of creativity within themselves, but it gets boxed in, suppressed, and shut off by the world in which they live and work. Inside the box, they have learned to approach problems with a rigidity of thought, but once they engage with the mixed-table process, they come into their full potential. Closed minds open up. Rigid thinking becomes more flexible.

Creatives inspire this in people and, in so doing, produce an environment in which people from all backgrounds can flourish, generating an energy and passion that didn't exist before. I've seen it time and time again, and it never ceases to amaze me.

HOSTING YOUR MIXED TABLE

The ideal size for a mixed-table meeting is around twenty-four people. I've found it most useful to have twelve creatives, nine subject-matter experts, and three thought leaders.

Weeks before the meeting convenes, clarify your objectives. What are you trying to achieve? What are the questions you're grappling with? It's a bit like painting a house. A good painter will spend time doing prep work; they don't just show up and start slapping paint on the walls. Instead, they wash off dirt or residue, scrape away cracked paint, and then prime the surface, which makes the difference between a botched job and a successful one.

Examine your motivations and make sure you are crystal clear on what you're trying to solve. Get specific. All of this will help you frame the question around overarching goals, rather than trying to figure out a goal on the spot.

Craft questions that clarify the specific problem set you're trying to address. Narrow your focus and don't aim too broadly. For example, "trying to solve world hunger" is too broad. Break it down to more specific problems within that larger arena to make it easier on yourself and genuinely achievable. Maybe you decide to focus on sub-Saharan countries, or a specific region within sub-Saharan Africa. Maybe you narrow it down to a specific city. The idea is to break down the challenge into manageable components.

Once you've clarified the problem, goals, and crafted some questions, convene a series of meetings over the course of three nights, which I recommend conducting offsite to ensure that people are away from office interruptions and distractions.

Below, I've designed a three-night Deep Applied Creativity™ session for you. As a practical matter, you can do this in a variety of ways. You can do two full days, four nights with one being social (which creates great bonding), or one day and two nights. In other words, you can slice and dice this. What doesn't work well are virtual sessions. There are two reasons for this. First, 80 percent of communication is nonverbal, and this is all about communication. Second, keeping people's attention *and* focus at the level they need to be is almost impossible in a digital format.

With that said, here's the structure of your Deep Applied Creativity™ session.

THE FIRST NIGHT

At the first meeting, you need to lay down some ground rules about what people can expect. Begin with introductions. Because the group is so diverse, it is likely that people don't know one another. When you start making introductions, people are going to be amazed.

After introductions, the second most important element of an effective mixed table is to feed people. *People love food.* It sounds facetious, perhaps, but a nice dinner helps people relax and get to know one another. Inevitably, some attendees will make strong connections right off the bat as a result.

Allow people time to enjoy dinner and chat. The next

steps don't come until afterward. Once finished, present them with a mini TED Talk-style presentation to introduce the problem at hand. For example, if the mixed table is about building a sales campaign for a product launch, bring a sales guru from the organization to give a presentation, during which time everyone learns the relevant data. Ideally, when introducing the subject, the presenter inspires people to think creatively about it.

This mini TED Talk has two primary goals:

- First, it orients the table around the specific subject matter for the evening, providing a broad perspective.
- Second, it informs and educates attendees in a way that is valuable to the outsiders (your creatives and thought leaders) while also engaging and stimulating insight.

After this initial presentation, divide participants into *three subgroups of equal size*, each comprised of creatives, subject-matter experts, and thought leaders. Appoint one person in each unit to lead the discussion. Generally, it's best for group leaders to be diplomatic yet firm in guiding discussions.

Give each subgroup an exercise, challenge, or question that is a subset of the overall question the mixed table is attempting to answer. For example, if the overall subject is about addressing hunger in a specific third-world country, one group might address the way local politics is exacerbating the problem, another might address the challenges of food distribution in the country, and a third might discuss economic hardships.

At this point, you might be wondering, "How long should I expect this to last?" If you start your meeting at 6:00 p.m., by the time you finish introductions and enjoy dinner, it will probably be close to 7:30 p.m. The initial presentation might last ten to fifteen minutes. Once you break into groups, give people an hour to talk.

Once the groups have come up with a solution, complicate the issue. Have them take a more granular approach. If the first group decides that the government should play a role in alleviating poverty, tell them to specify. "What would the government's campaign against hunger look like? What forms of communication would they use?" As they hone in on key points, instruct them to storyboard their solution so they end up with an explicit narrative for how to overcome the challenge.

At the conclusion of the evening, have each group give a fifteen- to thirty-minute presentation in which every member contributes. They should share their solution, followed by questions and answers to facilitate discussions with other groups.

There are *two rules* that govern the evening.

- First, every participant must agree to *discretion*. Discussions are to remain within the room. This creates a safe environment for people to speak openly. Sometimes, the information being discussed requires legal discretion, as in the case of the panels I've done around national security. Other times, the discretion is simply about ensuring that people can share what they really think without the risk of reprisal or recrimination.
- Second, *everyone present must participate* in the discussion. Everyone has something to say, and they must be willing to open up and share.

THE SECOND NIGHT

The second night allows for a deeper dive. Revise the questions from the previous night and have subgroups drill down into specific challenges. As an optional approach, the second night of the mixed table could deal with parallel applications. For instance, if the overarching subject is ending world hunger in a specific country, the second night might tackle the outbreak of a deadly strain of the flu in the region. Create examples prior to the meeting that have parallel applications for the same population or problem set.

Once the subgroups finish their discussion, they should

present their solution to the larger group. Have three presentations, one for each subgroup, limited to ten minutes each, and then give time for feedback. Afterward, you might send the subgroups back into discussion for another hour, so they can process that feedback. You could also give the subgroups new questions, so they can continue to refine and evolve their solutions. Alternatively, you could give homework, instructing them to research or create a visualization of the solution they've come up with.

THE THIRD NIGHT

On the third night, you want your groups to reach an outcome. You can adjust the questions depending on the discussions that have taken place the previous evenings if ideas are moving in a fruitful direction, but a big part of the third night is about taking ideas and turning them into actions. Subgroups should begin conceptualizing an operational approach, if applicable, to the challenges they've taken on. In the end, you need a path forward—a plan that can be translated into a campaign.

It's also important to give everyone a chance to provide feedback about the mixed table. What did they learn? What did they like or not like? Sometimes, after a mixed table, we create a private website so participants can stay in touch and continue the conversation, fostering an exchange of information and resources.

SURPRISING SOLUTIONS

In every mixed table I have experienced or heard about, people come up with wildly creative and innovative approaches to problem-solving. They always produce some original thought or idea, leading to insights or new advances. Watching this unfold is incredibly powerful.

At the same time, mixed tables sometimes validate an existing approach to a problem, which can be tremendously encouraging to leaders. "Your idea for tackling this problem is excellent. Continue to pursue it." This provides confirmation that the problem-solvers are on the right track. After the meeting, they can continue their work with renewed energy and enthusiasm.

By using the methodology presented in this chapter, you will get the most out of your mixed table, leveraging the power of divergent and disparate thinking to create surprising and transformational solutions for your organization. And the good news is this powerful tool is easy to implement.

WHY LEADERS DON'T CREATE MIXED TABLES

If it's so easy and effective, why doesn't every leader use a mixed-table approach to problem-solving?

There are at least eight reasons why leaders struggle to incorporate them:

1. They might not fully understand what a mixed table is. After all, you don't know what you don't know.
2. They've been affected by rigidity of thought. Sometimes, leaders assume they already know what they need to know, so they might not be looking for a more effective approach to problem-solving.
3. Some leaders suffer from a degree of intellectual laziness or exhaustion. The mixed-table process requires a lot of mental energy, which some leaders might be reluctant to expend.
4. They're interested in mixed tables, but they don't know how to begin bringing people together. Should they simply start flipping through their Rolodex and pulling out names? (The answer, by the way, is *yes*.)
5. They're too busy. Many leaders are so swamped with work and overwhelmed with responsibility that they can't make the mental space to approach their problems differently. To implement a mixed table, you have to be courageous enough to step back and reassess what you're doing.
6. Many leaders lack the confidence to approach their board of directors and say, "I want to invite a bunch of creative people to dinner and get them working on this problem set." Hopefully, the advice in this book will provide a clear-enough methodology to

help you feel confident about recommending this approach.

7. There's no guaranteed outcome. You can't control what people at a mixed table think any more than you can control what your teenager thinks. Looking at a problem from diverse perspectives certainly helps, but there's no guarantee that the discussion will produce the silver bullet you're looking for. Some leaders are reluctant to spend the time and effort to bring together a mixed table for three evenings when there is any degree of uncertainty.

8. They lack the budget. Chances are, when your organization crafted their annual budget, they didn't set aside a significant amount of money to pay for mixed tables. You have to pay and plan for meals, you might have to pay for travel expenses, you might have to pay speaking fees or honorariums for some participants or for a consultant. It adds up quickly.

All of these are valid concerns, but, in my estimation, none of them are compelling enough to reject the mixed-table approach. You have an opportunity to solve problems for yourself, your organization, and your community. You have a role to play in advancing society. This mixed-table methodology is the most effective way to do that, and with a bit of tenacity, courage, and determination, you can pull it off, no matter what obstacles are in the way.

THE METHODOLOGY OF A MIXED TABLE

Questions to Consider as You Assemble Your Team:

Who are the creative people you can invite to your mixed table? What subject-matter experts (SME) do you need? Who are some smart, accomplished *doers* (brilliant thought leaders) who you know?

Who would you consider the naysayers who might kill the initiative? Identify and avoid.

What reading material do you need to provide your team?

Have you established a nondisclosure agreement (NDA)? It's important to protect your organization and future solutions.

Questions to Consider as You Plan Each Session:

What is your ideal outcome from this session? Do you want to solve a problem? Do you want an idea of what the future looks like? Do you want to come up with multiple ideas, an executable plan? Is it realistic?

Why are you different in a meaningful way from your competition? What will be your competitors' approach to the market against you? How will tech or regulations affect or disrupt your industry? What can you do?

What are your potential results? Will it fix a pain point, bring about rewards, or avert a disaster?

What time and resources will you devote? What is the venue? You need a place where your team will not be regularly interrupted.

Tips for an Effective Mixed Table:

Plan the event over three successive nights after work and *serve a nice dinner*.

Introduce everyone sitting at the table.

After dinner, begin with a mini TED Talk to introduce the evening's problem.

After introducing the problem, split attendees into three smaller groups of approximately eight each.

Have each group deal with a different aspect of the overall problem. Make sure the problems are realistic but aggressive.

Assign individual group leaders to guide the discussion and make sure that everyone participates. (There are no bad ideas. There may be a few stupid ones, but that's fine.)

What happens in the room stays in the room. Insist upon discretion.

During the first night, present and discuss the problem. On the second night, consider discussing a parallel problem. On the third night, after you see where things are going, adjust your questions accordingly.

If your groups create an actionable goal, develop milestones to achieve it.

PART TWO

DEFINING, BUILDING, AND EXECUTING YOUR HIGH-IMPACT CAMPAIGN

Kinds of
Campaigns

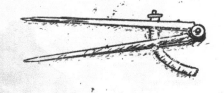

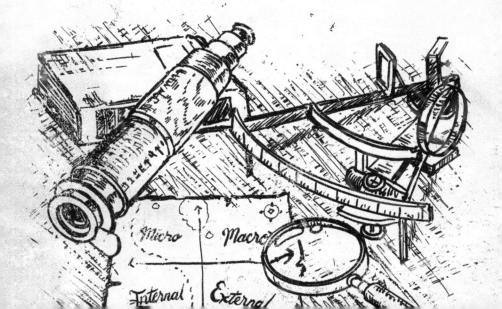

CHAPTER 5

———

THE DISCIPLINED CAMPAIGN

Your thoughts create your reality.

We run campaigns every day, even if we don't realize it. As I've mentioned before, one's entire *life* is a series of campaigns. Given my political background, I've spent my career thinking about campaigns more than most, but even I didn't realize how pervasive they were until a couple of years ago, when I hired branding coach Richard Janes.

Richard, who's now a good friend, has a gift for clarity when it comes to people and their true selves. I hired Richard when I was the CEO of MV because, on the surface, my career and life were successful but disconnected. I'd been a campaign manager, deputy assistant secretary of defense, CEO of a billion-dollar entity, and an entre-preneur. The issues I'd been involved in were equally as diverse, from stem cells to defense conversion in Russia to work with Hollywood on cutting-edge technologies to mobility and busing.

Richard forced me to do an exercise where I had to identify three words that describe me in *all* facets of my life. The first one was easy: impact. The second and third were harder to narrow down, though not for lack of options. There were plenty of *acceptable* words, but it took serious thought to find the *best* words—the ones that rang the truest. In the end, my three words were *impact*, *integrity*, and *insight*.

At the conclusion of the session, in his crisp London accent, Richard said, "John, this is brilliant! Don't you realize that everything you've done is about running campaigns? It ties together your business life, your gov-ernment life, your entrepreneurial life, everything. You should write a book about it."

And here we are!

Whether you're aiming to achieve personal or business-related goals, running well-structured campaigns is central to success. But what exactly is a campaign?

The dictionary definition is "a connected series of operations designed to bring about a particular result,"[8] which is rather broad but accurate. It's also a good starting point to understand how you can put your mixed-table solution to action, because the intersection between a fantastic mixed table and an effective campaign is where true magic occurs.

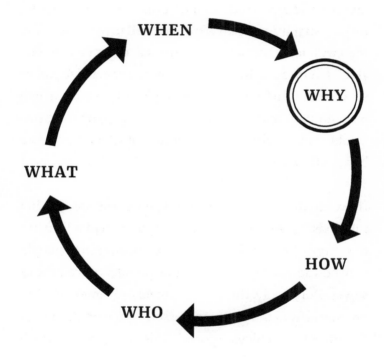

CAMPAIGNS THROUGH THE AGES

History is rife with military campaigns. Every great conqueror from Genghis Khan to Napoleon ran them.

---

8   "Campaign," *Merriam-Webster,* https://www.merriam-webster.com/dictionary/campaign (accessed September 19, 2018).

Even at the beginning of humanity, people were running campaigns, but the scope was incredibly narrow and centered on fulfilling the lowest levels of Maslow's hierarchy of needs.

In the Middle Ages, a time of stagnancy and repetition, knights and kings rode east on crusades, campaigning for Christianity. Women were expected to marry wealthy men with land and strong positions at court so as to provide for future children, and men were expected to gather their troops and come to the king's aid for war, which was rampant and frequent. Their campaigns were pre-established by virtue of the century in which they were born and evolved over time.

However, the personal campaigns people run today didn't fully exist until humanism gave way to individualism, for the surge of humanism didn't merely alter how people viewed the world; it altered how people viewed themselves. Put simply, this philosophical movement shifted emphasis from the divine to the self—from preparing for the afterlife to achieving goals in this life—through which internal campaigns became more incorporated into daily lives. People began setting aspirations and working to achieve personal goals in a manner that medieval civilization simply didn't allow or comprehend.

The English Renaissance itself started with a campaign

the day Henry VIII decided he'd rather marry Anne Boleyn than accept the status quo, subsequently campaigning to separate himself from the Catholic Church so he could legally divorce Catherine of Aragon. The implausibility of such an act might have been insurmountable two hundred years earlier, but with humanism on the rise and Florence paving a path of progressiveness, the king was able to achieve his goal.

While the wife-beheading Henry VIII is hardly a role model, he executed a massive campaign for himself, modeling a way of thinking that has percolated through subsequent generations. According to *The History Guide*'s Steven Kreis:

> That aspect of humanism which combated the sovereignty of tyrant, feudal lord, class, corporation, and tradition, has, for better or worse, had a tremendous influence upon the subsequent history of Europe. Indeed, it was during the humanist era that the freedom of individual expression and opposition to authority was first brought to the surface and became an integral part of the western intellectual tradition.[9]

In subsequent years, his daughter, Elizabeth, became Queen of England at a time when women were deemed

---

9   Steven Kreis, "Renaissance Humanism," *The History Guide*, February 6, 2016, http://www.historyguide.org/intellect/humanism.html.

unfit to rule. She was shrewd and savvy, and as such, "the adulation bestowed upon her both in her lifetime and in the ensuing centuries was not altogether a spontaneous effusion. It was the result of a carefully crafted, brilliantly executed campaign in which the queen fashioned herself as the glittering symbol of the nation's destiny."[10] Given the reverence society treats her with to this day, her campaign was highly successful.

Later, post-humanism, President Thomas Jefferson commissioned Lewis and Clark to explore and map the Louisiana Purchase. To do so, they developed a campaign plan that involved understanding their context, mapping their environment and route, developing a series of strategies, arming those strategies with tactics, and executing. It took them three years of traversing waterways and hiking overland to reach the Pacific. Along the way, they encountered numerous obstacles, including harsh winter weather, illness, an occasional lack of food, loss of their horses, and diplomatic struggles with various Native American tribes. Their campaign helped them deal with the unexpected and keep moving toward their goal.

On November 7, 1805, they succeeded, coming in sight of the Pacific Ocean near the mouth of the Columbia River. They had little food, the area was wracked with storms,

---

10 John S. Morrill and Stephen J. Greenblatt, "Elizabeth I," *ENCYCLOPÆDIA BRITANNICA*, accessed September 19, 2018, https://www.britannica.com/biography/Elizabeth-I.

and another harsh winter set in, but they'd made it. Now, they had a second campaign to run: the whole damn thing in reverse.

Today, as a result of humanism, we have the ability and authority to run micro and macro, external and internal campaigns. People are able to think holistically and do intentionally. As we can see, we're all blind to the limitations of our times, but it goes without saying that the possibilities we face today are vastly different. We can do virtually anything. Try telling Elon Musk otherwise.

Today, campaigns cover an endless array of industries, subjects, and fields of study: politics, science, military, sales, fund-raising, marketing, public awareness, lobbying, social media, security, book drives, recycling, entrepreneurial, public health, safety, technology, mindfulness, education, mergers and acquisitions, and more.

How we strive to achieve those campaigns is what becomes muddled and mired in day-to-day life, limiting our efficiency and possibly even undermining the very objective we set out to achieve.

Breaking that process down is our next focus.

MICRO AND MACRO CAMPAIGNS

By and large, campaigns fall into one of four categories. Before we go through these, it is important to set a few baseline definitions.

For purposes of this construct, "internal" (or "intra") means either *specific to an individual* or *within an entire organization*. "External" (or "inter") means you are ultimately trying to compel an action outside of one's direct control.

"Micro" versus "macro" is a matter of scale. When narrowly focused, we are impacting either a small number of individuals or impacting individuals minimally. When focused on large-scale impact, we are talking "macro."

In the table below, these definitions mean that the y-axis is "quantitative" in that it's the scale of the campaign, and the x-axis is the internal versus external.

Campaign *noun* /kam'pān/

An organized course of action to
achieve a particular goal.

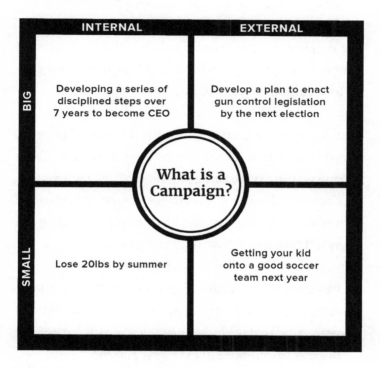

- Campaigns are broken up into many different types
  and should always include a time frame.

- Can you think of any campaign examples
  you've run without knowing it?

- **Internal Micro Campaigns.** These are smaller, narrowly focused goals. Example: *"I'm going to knock out all my errands on Saturday morning."*

The majority of the campaigns in our lives are internal micro campaigns, which include all the little things we try to accomplish in our daily lives.

Your Saturday errands to-do list is a series of internal micro campaigns. Every one of the items on it, from picking up the dry cleaning to going to the grocery store, requires thought. If you want to get all your errands done in time for cocktails, minimizing stoplights, avoiding too many left turns, this requires a campaign.

- **Internal Macro Campaigns.** These are larger, long-term goals we strive for. Example: *"Over the next two years, we want to reduce our healthcare costs by 5 percent in order to improve EBITDA by X percent."*

Reaching this goal requires a holistic approach such as negotiating with healthcare providers, increasing wellness within the workforce, the inclusion of hardware like personal fitness devices, lobbying policymakers for fewer healthcare mandates, and so on.

- **External Micro Campaign.** These rely on others for successful completion even though they're narrowly focused. Example: *"I am going to help my daughter get into a good college."*

If that's your goal, you'll probably be in full campaign mode by the time she's a freshman in high school. You've mapped the process—if you want your daughter to attend the University of Wisconsin, you know that as an in-state resident she's going to need a 3.8 GPA and a 31 on her ACT, as well as a certain number of extracurricular activities to increase her chance of being accepted. As she goes through high school, you will track and adjust her performance in light of these criteria, using various tactics of effective parenting.

- **External Macro Campaign.** These are large-scale efforts that rely on and/or impact many people. Example: *"We're going to reduce violent extremism in the Arab world."*

This requires a complex multifaceted plan including military engagement, diplomacy, messaging, customization, targeting, coordination, and significant funding.

Let's be honest. We could write a whole book on this alone. The point here is when you're trying to make a big change that is as far-reaching as every corner of the globe, you still need a campaign.

We humans spend the vast majority of our time on internal micro and external macro campaigns, but the other two, internal macro and external micro, are equally as important, and frequently overlooked.

It may seem obvious, but the creative thought provided by a mixed table is probably not necessary for most micro campaigns, though you might consider them a value-add in some situations. Macro campaigns, on the other hand, need diverse creative thinking, and including a mixed table will surely set you apart from your competition or your peers.

"ON" VERSUS "IN"

You have to work "on" something before you work "in" something. When seeking the best answer to a question, you're working *on* the answer. That's your mixed table. When implementing the answer, you're *in* the campaign.

Put another way, a mixed table can be seen as the "inward-facing" phase of a campaign because it centers *on* planning and creating a solution set. Conversely, the "outward-facing" phase involves implementing your solutions. At that point, you're *in* the campaign.

Suppose you're the CEO of a food-processing company. You've seen a competitor take a hit from an incident involving tainted beef, and you want to ensure that your company avoids making the same mistakes, so you convene a mixed table involving your team and a few outside experts to discuss ways you can create the safest possible processes. This is the inward-facing phase; you're working *on* the problem.

Once your mixed table has outlined a solution set, you assemble an external team to implement it: the outward-facing phase, working *in* the campaign.

TEAMS TO IMPLEMENT SOLUTIONS

When it comes to executing a campaign, I recommend creating a different kind of team than the one you had for your mixed table. You no longer need a diverse array of thinkers unless your goal specifically calls for it. At this point, it's more important to create a team that can successfully execute the campaign, such as a group of people with highly similar skills and expertise.

For instance, there's no doubt in my mind that the decision to go after bin Laden wasn't made by the SEAL Team; they were the implementers working in the campaign. The decision was made by a series of policymakers, starting with the president and going down from there based upon rigorous analysis by the intelligence community. That information and the decision were then transferred to the SEAL Team to execute—working *on* the problem versus *in* the campaign.

In regard to external macro campaigns, given their extreme level of complexity, your team will have an outsized impact on whether or not you're successful, so choose members wisely.

Assembling the campaign team begins the second you have your solution set in place, but you won't finalize the team until you've mapped the context of your campaign. My suggestion is to identify the right kind of experts for the problem you're attempting to solve.

This is a dynamic process. You might realize you need specific kinds of expertise as you develop your strategy. However, as the old business saying goes, "You hire for talent and fire for culture." People can have great résumés and the right skills, but I always find it best to involve those who fit into the culture at large; if they don't, they won't be assets.

Steps of a
Campaign

SIX STEPS TO A CAMPAIGN

When putting together your campaign, consider these six essential steps. In the coming chapters, we will look at each step in detail. By way of introduction, they are the following:

1. Deciding on your **outcome**.
2. Understanding the **context** of your campaign.
3. **Mapping** the process.
4. Developing a dynamic **strategy** to execute your campaign.
5. Specifying **tactics** to carry out the strategy.
6. **Execution**!

Outcomes

CHAPTER 6

———

STEP 1: DEFINE YOUR OUTCOME

If you don't know where you're going, you're going to end up somewhere else.

> **THINK ABOUT THESE TERMS WHEN CONSIDERING THE OUTCOME**
>
> Goal, Objective, End State/End Result, Vision, Conclusion, Target, Mission, Aspiration, Desire/Hope, Purpose, Dream, Intention

When I was a junior in high school, my father gave me a book called *If You Don't Know Where You're Going, You'll Probably End Up Somewhere Else* by David Campbell. Originally published in the 1970s, it was geared toward younger generations, but as the times changed, Campbell evolved the concept to appeal to a broader adult audience and has since republished the book twice, in 1997 and 2009. His idea, as the title indicates, is both simple and vital: if you haven't articulated your goals, you won't achieve them.

Do you know what you want to achieve? Have you defined your desired outcome as clearly as possible? Failing to do so has been the downfall of many organizations and individuals.

Deepak Chopra, MD, calls this the power of intention. What are you intentionally trying to accomplish?

I don't mean to keep picking on Kodak, but they provide a perfect case study, and I do wonder how such an iconic brand lost its way. Kodak wasn't simply a successful business, but a pioneering business *leader*, responsible for many advances in early photography, as I discussed earlier. The name Kodak became synonymous with photography. So, what went wrong?

I believe the answer may be profoundly simple. The executives didn't have the right outcome in mind. They should have been committed to providing customers the most technologically advanced and easy-to-use photography tools. As a cutting-edge company, they should have *stayed* on the cutting edge. Instead, they continued proliferating old photographic chemicals and film even in the face of the digital era's ascendance.

For decades, Kodak innovated as a company, and then they simply stopped, fading away into obscurity. In the end, they lost market share, their reputation, and their dominance of an entire industry.

Their objectives didn't keep pace with the times, so they ceased serving customer desires—and they're not the only ones. Of the companies that made up the Fortune 500 list in 1955, only sixty remained by 2016.[11] Did any of these companies set out to fail? Did their leaders decide to stop serving customers?

"I think our goal for the year should be to lose market dominance and fail to meet changing customer demand," said no CEO ever.

It's quite possible these companies lacked the perspective to pinpoint what they needed to do, and consequently, they failed to identify the best objectives to progress with the times.

In some sectors, it's easy to have clear objectives. For instance, on the surface, a political campaign has the easiest outcome to define. When someone runs for public office, there's no confusion that the objective is to win

---

11   Mark J. Perry, "Fortune 500 Firms 1955 v. 2016," *AEI Ideas*, December 13, 2016, http://www.aei.org/publication/fortune-500-firms-1955-v-2016-only-12-remain-thanks-to-the-creative-destruction-that-fuels-economic-prosperity/.

the election. On Election Day, campaign staffers and politicians sprint at ninety-five miles an hour to reach the finish line. At the end of the race, they either won or lost.

However, the politician's road may continue. Just because she lost doesn't mean she'll never achieve her true goals, for if you dig deeper, you'll often find many politicians have other motivations for running beyond simply "winning." Maybe she wants to advance a policy, try to change certain laws, or fight to maintain the status quo. One politician might run for office in order to undo the Affordable Care Act, while another runs to preserve it. These are the real goals they want to achieve, and becoming an elected official is a strategy to achieve them.

In the business world, objectives change with the times or circumstances, and leaders who fail to perceive these changes can find themselves pouring all of their energy into reaching the wrong outcome. By the time they realize it, the damage is done, and it might be too late to redirect toward a different goal.

LEARNING FROM MISTAKES

One of the biggest disruptions in Western civilization stems from the Catholic Church losing its hold over society during the Renaissance. Why? Truthfully, a thousand reasons. But at the core, the church's goal was to maintain dominance over everything and everybody, and during the Middle Ages, when people spent their lives planning for the afterlife, the church was ostensibly able to do this.[12] Religious leaders didn't believe the church's role was to cater to the people. The people catered to *them*.

With the rise of humanism, the first true propagation of the written word, and people beginning to think for themselves, the church didn't realize how empowered people had become until it was too late. King Henry VIII declared he no longer required their authority, Martin Luther wrote the "Ninety-Five Theses" that sparked the Protestant Reformation, and the English warred over religion for centuries to come. Roughly five hundred years have passed, and the Catholic Church still hasn't regained the power it once had—not that they should—but their inability to adapt with the times lost them authority and power forever (so far).

Just as I believe we should learn from what the greats in the Renaissance achieved, there's plenty to learn from their failures too, and the importance of setting objectives that cater to the needs and desires of the people.

---

12   Alixe Bovey, "Church in the Middle Ages: From Dedication to Dissent." *The British Library*, January 17, 2014, www.bl.uk/the-middle-ages/articles/church-in-the-middle-ages-from-dedication-to-dissent.

THE FIVE WHYS

Setting the right goal is central to success within this construct—it all flows downhill from there—but how do you know when you have the correct goal? It's not easy. Everything moves so fast these days, our senses are constantly being assaulted by data, and incoming leaders must be disciplined about forcing themselves to move toward deeper insights when setting goals.

That means the very aha moment when you first think you've determined your goal needs to be challenged.

Enter Taiichi Ohno of Toyota Motor Corporation, who developed a concept called the "Five Whys" to aid in the process of goal setting. It begins with a problem such as, "My car stopped on the way home from work."

Now, ask a series of five "why" questions to get to the root cause and identify your objective.

1. Why did my car stop on the way home from work? Because I ran out of gas.
2. Why did I run out of gas? Because I didn't put any gas in the tank on the way to work this morning.
3. Why didn't I put any gas in the tank this morning? Because I don't have any money.
4. Why don't you have any money? Because I lost it all on a bad investment.

5. Why did you make such a bad investment? Because I listened to my shady cousin Larry's investment advice.

Asking yourself the "Five Whys" after your initial aha moment forces you toward deeper insight and understanding. The example above may be tongue-in-cheek, but the concept is spot-on. This tool helps clarify your specific objective or reveals that you nailed it the first time.

The "Five Whys" is also an excellent conversation starter at a mixed table.

WHY PEOPLE GET MUDDLED

Leaders have a plethora of decisions to make, with a bunch more incoming every day. We can't always take the time to be thoughtful. I recall an incident in which a member of my lobbying firm wanted to exit a partner, so he made it his primary objective. It was a strategic play but not a thoughtful one.

The overall objectives of the firm were to increase revenue, create a fair distribution of the workload, and boost client satisfaction. Exiting a partner didn't contribute to any of these, but in a fast-paced environment, he saw it as a smart tactical move. This is where so many leaders stumble. I know I certainly have. They make decisions on the fly, rather than stepping back, analyzing the situation, and taking a methodical approach.

In the late 1960s, pioneering psychologists Dr. Edwin Locke and Dr. Gary Latham identified five goal-setting components that will improve the chances of success for any individual or organization. Locke and Latham assert you need these components in order to define your outcome.

I think this is a good tool for developing your goals. When I created my model, I used slightly different words, but the concepts were generally the same.

The five components are as follows:

1. Clarity
2. Commitment
3. Feedback
4. Challenge
5. Task complexity

Breaking these down, you should pursue outcomes that are *crystal clear* not only to you, but to those around you, so everyone understands exactly what you're trying to achieve. Part of clarity entails writing it down. My view on the world is that we all have an exponentially better chance at accomplishing something if we write it down with regularity and specificity.

The next component, and one I'm in complete alignment with, is *commitment*. To state the obvious, one has to be committed to getting something done in order to do so. It's as simple as that. If you're not committed to it, don't do it.

Feedback is the other component that really resonates with me. At every stage of executing a campaign, whether it's contextualizing, mapping, strategy, tactics, or execution, there has to be feedback and an understanding of what the desired outcome is.

Challenge, on the other hand, is a little gray. Some outcomes are big challenges that will stretch you, but within a campaign, even those outcomes that aren't big challenges require clear thought. To me, challenge is not a necessary condition when defining one's outcome. The same logic applies to *task complexity*, though that doesn't mean either one is unimportant.

Consider your objectives in light of these five components to ensure that you're on the right track. If you're struggling to gain clarity on your objective, use a mixed table and let a holistic perspective refine your focus. Combine the five goal-setting principles with the "Five Whys," and use your mixed-table breakout groups to tackle the problem with a thoughtful, multidisciplinary approach.

LET'S BE REASONABLE

The objective you set might be admirable, but it should also be reasonable. Someone might say his objective is to become an NBA star, but if he lacks the athletic prowess, years of training, and body conditioning, it's unlikely to happen. Idealism is great, but when you select your objectives, it's best to use a rational filter.

As lauded as da Vinci is today, believe it or not, he never fully executed some of his grand plans in life, believing himself a failure upon his deathbed. As Michael J. Gelb notes in *How to Think Like Leonardo da Vinci*, "Leonardo saw that he would die without fully realizing his dream of unifying all knowledge."[13] He hoped to combine and publish his wide range of notes on philosophy, science, and art, which he never did. Da Vinci's goal was simply unmanageable. Combining all knowledge was impossible for one person to accomplish at that time, even for someone as phenomenal as da Vinci.

Conversely, the objective can't be so easy to attain that it provides no challenge. One of my personal goals is to try one new thing every year of my life. I've had the goal for

13   Michael J. Gelb, *How to Think Like Leonardo da Vinci* (New York: Delacorte Press, 1998), 38.

ages, and I believe it keeps me young and nimble-minded. Last year, at fifty-seven years old, I learned how to paddleboard. I don't feel a need to jump out of an airplane or do anything crazy, but I continue to push myself to try things I've never done before.

One of my specific goals is to bicycle all over Europe in the upcoming years. Eventually, I'd love to reach every country on the continent. To do that, I'm training, planning, and budgeting for it. Ultimately, it's an ongoing goal that I'm working on little by little each year. I went on a biking trip last year, and I'm planning another one next year.

It's a difficult objective, but it's achievable. It will take a lot of hard work over a number of years, but I can get there as long as I stay in shape, budget properly, and keep working at it. I've set a hard-enough objective that I feel challenged by it, but it's not so extreme that I feel overwhelmed. If I'd said, "I want to ride my bicycle to the peak of the world's seven tallest mountains," it would be irrational, and I might be setting myself up for discouragement. If a mixed table recommended that objective, hopefully I would run it through a rational filter before committing to it.

At the same time, my goal is specific. I didn't say, "I want to bicycle through a whole bunch of countries all over the place." I narrowed my focus. "I want to ride my bicycle through every European country during the next decades of my life."

I have *clarity* on my goal. It's *challenging* enough to keep me interested. I'm willing to *commit* to the years of hard work it will take to achieve. As I plan and execute biking trips, I gain *feedback* I can use to adjust my approach. The task is *complex* enough to be exciting without overwhelming me. All things considered, I have an excellent chance of achieving my objective.

NARROW YOUR GOAL AND WRITE IT DOWN

The more specific and definable you can make your objective, the easier it will be to measure if you've achieved it. As mentioned earlier, you have to make sure of one thing: that your objective is written down.

From Napoleon Hill to Stephen Covey, many motivational speakers have talked about the importance of writing down your goals and objectives once you've established them, the idea being to keep them foremost in your mind. This allows you to constantly refresh your thinking and reorient yourself toward your objective. In his book *Think and Grow Rich*, Napoleon Hill recommends reading it to yourself out loud twice a day—once in the morning and once at night—while also visualizing yourself making it happen.

In the end, your goal should be SMART: Specific, Measurable, Attainable, Relevant, Time-Bound. Let your mixed table help you. Once your goal is in place, write it down and keep it in a prominent location. Continue to think about it, weigh your actions against it, and regularly sift through feedback as your campaign unfolds.

SET AN END DATE

It's important to set a fixed date for your objective. In fact, that should be the starting point for your schedule. Set an end date and work backward from there. For example, when I set out to write this book, I established a desired publication date. Afterward, I discussed the plan with my publishing company and marketing team, asking key questions, "What do we need to do to reach my desired publication date? What does the marketing team need to do to ensure public awareness? Which social media platform should they create for me?"

Every time a book is published, a campaign is created. People might not necessarily have an end date, but I found it useful, as it has helped me complete the book in an efficient and timely manner.

Selecting a date might seem arbitrary, and that's fine. The point is to hold yourself and your team accountable. Pick a date that feels rational based on what you can make happen, and don't be afraid to make it a bit challenging. It can provide that last boost of motivation.

Once your objective is clear and your end date is set, it's time to map your context, which we'll delve into in the following chapter.

CLARIFY YOUR OUTCOME

What's your desired outcome? If necessary, use the "Five Whys" to clarify. Write down your desired outcome and put it somewhere you can look at it every day. Be as specific as possible. Remember, it takes constant vigilance to achieve it.

Does your objective have Locke and Latham's five components (Clarity, Commitment, Feedback, Challenge, Task Complexity)?

Is your goal SMART (Specific, Measurable, Attainable, Relevant, Time-Bound)?

What's your timeline? Specifically, what is your end date?

Understanding
Context

CHAPTER 7

STEP 2: UNDERSTANDING THE CONTEXT

Even if you understand the context, you can't plan for everything.

> **THINK ABOUT THESE TERMS WHEN CONSIDERING CONTEXT**
>
> Frame, Environment, Intelligence, Circumstance, Reference, Situation, Position, Backdrop, Background, Conditions, Scene, Setting, Milieu, the Dynamic

Context is an often-underrated critical component of success.

The Renaissance was born out of the context of the time, revolutionary thinking hinging upon the changing world.

The plague had decimated a third of Europe, the printing press was on the rise, and a return to Greek philosophy ignited a new wave of thinking. The Medicis capitalized on the changing times by embarking on a quest to re-create Florence, which they likely never could have done if the context of the time had been different.

As for da Vinci, by the time he was born, the Renaissance was already blossoming in Florence, making it possible for him to embark on his artistic, philosophical career. If Michelangelo had wanted to sculpt nude, muscular men four hundred years prior, he likely would have never been discovered.

What these examples make clear is that without understanding the context, we can't possibly run effective campaigns.

THE STEM CELL WARS

In 2006, before we began our stem cell campaign, Michael J. Fox and I carefully examined the political context we were stepping into. Michael has a brilliant political mind, and I dived deeply into the subject. We needed to understand the balance of power in Washington and the upcoming congressional elections, including the fact that general opinion agreed Democrats were likely to regain the House of Representatives but not the Senate.

President George W. Bush had won reelection, and we knew the incumbent president's party typically experiences a six-year itch, which is to say, they lose seats in that last midterm election. Ostensibly, momentum was in our favor, and we were also aware that patient advocacy groups had a lot of pent-up energy. They were frustrated by the lack of stem cell research and President Bush's opposition to funding it. Though it was a fairly complex arena of scientific study, a lot of awareness had already been generated in the public about the subject.

Back then, the public highly regarded celebrity advocates such as Michael J. Fox, Christopher Reeves, and Mary Tyler Moore. The context seemed perfect to use this wedge issue to impact upcoming Senate races, so we chose our objective accordingly. It was a deliberate and thoughtful decision based on the specific situation in which we were working—that's the key.

Additionally, in 2006, Michael J. Fox's path to success had been inadvertently cleared by Rush Limbaugh, who went on the air and made the ludicrous claim that Michael was putting on a show by failing to take his meds so that his Parkinson's symptoms would be more dramatic on TV ads. In reality, Michael's dyskinesia, the involuntary body swaying and writhing, during the filming of the TV ads was a *direct result* of his medication, not evidence that he had intentionally neglected to take it.

We were able to use Limbaugh's false claims against him. We let momentum build for a few days, then Michael came out swinging on the *CBS Evening News*. For thirteen minutes out of seventeen minutes of news airtime, he set the record straight with Katie Couric. After that, we hit one news program after another, including the *Today* show, *This Week with George Stephanopoulos,* and *Anderson Cooper 360*. In the end, this media tour, the public feud with Limbaugh, and the publicity it generated for stem cell research created a wedge issue that was largely credited for flipping the Senate in a sweeping victory for the Democratic Party, the party more favorable to stem cell research.

In today's "so what?" context, it's quite possible that most people would simply shrug off Michael J. Fox's media tour. At best, it would be a lot more arduous to generate the same amount of public attention. Someone trying to pursue an analogous campaign today would have to carefully consider the current context and map a different series of steps to achieve a similar objective, as the political and social contexts have so drastically changed.

The public is quicker to dismiss celebrity advocacy, so they no longer carry the weight they once did. Fake news has also become far more prevalent, so people don't know whom to trust, and, alarmingly, the general public more readily latches on to outrageous conspiracy theories.

Context is about understanding the environment in which you operate and live.

The Apollo program, for instance, changed the context around which we perceived Earth. Also known as Project Apollo, the Apollo program was the third United States human spaceflight program conducted by NASA. As most Americans alive in the 1960s will remember, it resulted in humans landing on the Moon for the first time.

From the far reaches of space, astronaut-geologist Harrison Schmitt took a photo, later dubbed the "Blue Marble." As noted by *The Guardian*'s Christopher Riley, "For 40 years [that image] has been used to change minds, behaviors and political policies."[14] We saw the world as a fragile entity for the first time in human history, forever altering our context.

It fundamentally shifted society, ultimately fueling today's environmental movement, which people wouldn't have had the same understanding for in the early 1960s, mere years before the Apollo program launched.

Let's consider a much starker example. In the early days of Hollywood, it was perfectly acceptable for white actors

---

14   Christopher Riley, "Apollo 40 Years On: How the Moon Missions Changed the World For Ever," *Guardian*, December 16, 2012, https://www.theguardian.com/science/2012/dec/16/apollo-legacy-moon-space-riley.

to play black characters. It was abhorrent, but the context of the time accepted it. Go back a few centuries to Elizabethan times: women weren't allowed to become actors, so men portrayed the female roles, as captured in *Shakespeare in Love*. While all of this sounds ludicrous to contemporary ears, it was normal in other time periods. This doesn't make the acts morally right, but it does mean people working in those environments would have to consider the context when formulating a strategy.

Thirty years ago, if you were running late for a meeting, you were just late. You didn't have a cell phone, so you couldn't send a text. You didn't even have email. Letting people know you were going to be late to a meeting was much more difficult, so people might cut you some slack. Today, there would be no excuse for not at least texting to let people know you're running behind. This might seem like a small thing, but it's a different context. You have to operate accordingly in order to get things done.

TIME, SPACE, AND MATTER

Framing the context in which you are pursuing your objective is ultimately about three factors: time, space, and matter. This is the definition of reality. By understanding the time in which your campaign exists, the space in which it exists, and the material reality, you can clarify the environment and adjust accordingly.

Consider Donald Trump's race to the White House. His target decision-makers were the voters, but he clearly understood the context in which he was campaigning. He perceived that it was a time, place, and environment of populism, something Hillary Clinton and her team seemed to miss, and he played to this idea in his speeches. While many were appalled at some of the things he said and did, it worked within the context of the time.

Consider the students in Florida who, in light of yet another tragic school shooting, perceived a context in which they could campaign for a modest amount of gun control. How effective this campaign will prove to be remains to be seen, but the students have clearly identified their target decision-makers (politicians) and the broader context (time, space, matter) in society.

In both of these examples, the campaign team may or may not have understood the context intellectually, but they at least understood it instinctively, and they campaigned accordingly. In Trump's case, this led to a surprising (some would say, shocking) win.

INTELLIGENCE MATTERS

Intelligence is an important part of context, and in business and government, you think about the intelligence around your adversaries constantly using market research and competitive analysis, looking at how your clients interact in the marketplace.

It's not just what you can see and know today; it's a broader picture of what could throw your campaign off course. What are the disruptions, trends, circumstances, innovations, and regulations or inhibitors that you face? All of this intelligence and analyses are part of context.

DIG INTO THE DATA

Gathering data to understand your context tends to cause the most frustration because some of the information you seek won't be readily available.

Ultimately, you just have to dig as far into the data as you can, accepting that you will not uncover every last kernel of knowledge. Even so, do your best to build as much data as you can into the context of your campaign.

Thanks to tech and big data, organizations with the resources can now access a universe of tools to learn about their audience's needs, likes, and behavior patterns. Pulling together all of that information will be helpful in the long run even if it doesn't answer every question you have at the time.

Answer as many questions as possible about your context, but eventually you will reach a point of diminishing returns. When you get to that point, it's time to stop collecting data and map your process. As long as you have a good sense of who your target decision-makers are, you will have the clarity you need.

QUESTIONS FOR UNDERSTANDING YOUR CONTEXT

What's the social environment around your objective?

What's the political context in which you will operate?

How does the media discuss the issue?

What are the controversies or contentions in the general public related to the issue?

Mapping
the Process

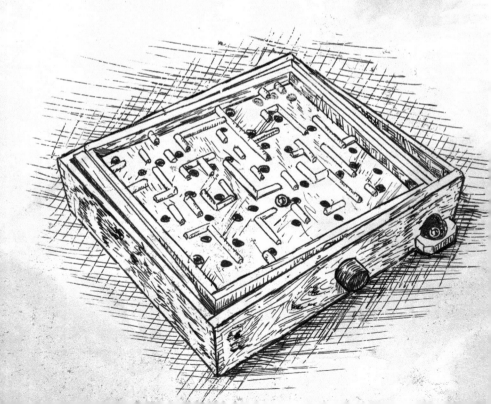

CHAPTER 8

STEP 3: MAPPING THE PROCESS

Don't be on the road to nowhere.

> ### THINK ABOUT THESE TERMS WHEN CONSIDERING MAPPING
>
> Surveying, Planning, Diagraming, Outlining, Charting

By now, you have the "why" of your objective. Now, you get to map it.

Mapping the process to achieve your goal means figuring out the *who, what, when, where,* and *how.* Inevitably, these will entail decision-makers and enterprise processes. We can't avoid them, so we might as well accept them and do ourselves a favor by understanding the decision-makers and processes within which they operate.

Every organization is filled with processes, so if you want to sell a product or service, be ready to understand and navigate them.

Let's pick on the government because I know it well. Working on an objective within government might seem simple at first—identify the person or persons who need your service, make sure that person has the money to meet the need and the authority to use the money, then ensure that he or she has a contracting vehicle. That's it.

Except, it's not.

People spend their entire careers working on those three steps because each of them is extraordinarily complex, partly due to the sheer amount of bureaucratic red tape and partly because of the number of people involved in the decision-making process.

Then, of course, we must understand the flow of money. The president creates a budget, and Congress authorizes it and appropriates the funding. The president then signs that budget into law. After that, money is directed from the Treasury to the Office of Management and Budget (OMB), which distributes the money to comptrollers in each relevant federal agency. The comptrollers distribute that money within their agencies to department and program managers, who further divide the money. Only then is the money actually applied to specific contracts, and it makes its way down to the contractors.

This doesn't even touch on how Congress appropriates funds, a complex process that involves subcommittees in the House and Senate hearings. Often, Congress goes back and forth with the administration on the budget. Then, the budget goes into a full House or Senate committee, and from there, it is voted on by the House and Senate. If it passes both the House and Senate, it goes to a jurisdiction subcommittee, back to final reconciliation between the House and Senate, and then to a final vote of both. Only then does it arrive on the president's desk for a signature.

The next hurdle? The timeline. When does the president submit his budget? When does Congress act on the budget? When are the hearings? When does the budget get signed into law? When does the money trickle down from the OMB to the comptrollers and then to particular contracts? It's best to apprehend all of this so you can determine when and where you can influence that budget and where the money goes.

When you finally obtain your funding, you'll want a clear sense of the procurement process. Typically, the government has to issue a contract, such as an indefinite delivery/indefinite quantity contract (IDIQ), a Broad

Agency Announcement (BAA), sole source, or whatever the multitude of other contracting vehicles are.

Simply writing all of that is exhausting. Actually monitoring the steps in relation to a business deal? Even more so. All of these processes are extremely complicated, just as in most large organizations. The bigger the system, the more rigid the processes tend to be, so in achieving an objective, I find mapping it out saves me time and stress. It helps me develop a deeper understanding of what, precisely, needs to happen. Otherwise, how can I devise an effective campaign?

My brain goes to government because it's complicated and I know it really well, but don't misunderstand me—mapping is an essential part of the process, whether it's for government or the private sector.

Consider transportation companies that move volatile chemicals and other materials across state lines. This is a multibillion-dollar industry annually, and the process of getting the correct safety certifications, state licenses, and contract vehicles in place makes the difference between success and failure for large employers, not to mention the operators who drive their trucks in order to feed their families.

Fortunately, some procedures are quite easy. Getting your

child onto a community soccer team is simple. Enrolling them in a nice preschool might be a bit harder. Helping them get accepted by an Ivy League school is very tough. In every instance, understanding the process is key to creating an effective strategy.

THE SPECIFIC STEPS

No matter what sort of campaign you're running, no matter what field, industry, or arena it's in, you are ultimately trying to convince *someone* to do *something*.

Even during the Renaissance, a time when the quest for truth and beauty supposedly surmounted all base thinking, artists relied upon decision-makers to continue creating. They needed patrons to support them and the public to endorse them by fawning over and purchasing their work. With burgeoning consumerism, the public had true power for the first time in modern Western civilization and could determine whether or not an artist was able to continue pursuing creative passions.

In many respects, not much has changed today, with the Renaissance patron somewhat equal to a Hollywood studio. No matter the field, we will encounter such decision-makers. In any large organization, there are always multiple individuals involved in decision-making, which means there are always numerous decision-makers or stakeholders. Navigating who has authority around any particular need can be difficult, but it's also important to identify who *influences* those individuals.

To understand your context, map the decision-making process step by step. In reaching your objective, clarify who can say *yes* and who can say *no*.

In my campaign with Michael J. Fox, we needed key senators to vote yes on funding stem cell research. In order to get those yes votes, we needed voters in key elections to say yes to the right candidates. Clarifying this allowed us to devise a strategy for reaching the right people (I used the "Five Whys" as part of this process).

Once you identify the decision-makers, clarify their motivations, needs, and budget. Do you have any existing ties to them? These can be leveraged during your campaign. Other aspects that can affect your campaign include individual dynamics, the stability of the decision-makers, their knowledge about the subject, and their job security or lack thereof.

As I mentioned, it's also important to consider who influences your decision-makers. Often, they are just as important as the people wielding the more obvious power.

Consider Leonardo da Vinci at the beginning of his career.

Like most young artists, he trained under a gifted expert, Andrea del Verrocchio (1435–88), who received patronage from Lorenzo de' Medici. Verrocchio had his own livelihood to tend to and couldn't become a patron of da Vinci, but he had influence with other decision-makers in the community. Fortunately for Leonardo, Verrocchio adored his work, famously allowing him to paint the angel on his masterpiece *Baptism of Christ*, and subsequently vowing "never to touch colors again."[15] Ultimately, this mentorship mattered, as his patron Lorenzo de' Medici helped shape Leonardo's career.

TARGET THE ANTIBODIES

What if Verrocchio had balked at Leonardo's work? Sometimes decision-influencers are antibodies, meaning they work against your particular objective. Even if they're merely neutral, it still requires moving them from neutral to positive, turning an antibody into a probiotic who will help you achieve your objective.

Are there any antibodies involved in the decision-making process you're navigating?

Senators opposing stem cell research were antibodies for us. Michael J. Fox and I knew we would have to work

---

15   Michael J. Gelb, *How to Think Like Leonardo da Vinci* (New York: Delacorte Press, 1998), 89.

around them, somehow get past them, or possibly convince them to join our cause.

In some instances, we have to pass through gatekeepers in order to reach our target audience. Do you know who they are? For example, if you attempt to transform a run-down neighborhood, your target decision-makers are local politicians, but first you have to get approved for a grant to fund the project. In that case, the people who have the grant money are gatekeepers on the path to your objective.

The opposite of an antibody is a "probiotic," people or organizations who *help* your target decision-makers move closer to your objective—the Andrea del Verrocchios of the world. Pinpoint these people because they will almost certainly play an essential role in your strategy. In our stem cell campaign, the pro-stem cell advocates had certain supportive politicians who served as champions, or probiotics, in Congress as we navigated the complex processes.

Context and mapping help form and inform which strategies you'll need. They are necessary components to a complete campaign.

QUESTIONS FOR MAPPING YOUR PROCESS

What is the decision-making process for your objective outcome? What are specific steps in the process?

Who are the decision-makers? What do you know about them? Do you have ties to them?

Are you fixing their pain? Helping them avoid something they fear? Giving them something they desire?

If budgets are involved, what intelligence do you have on their budget?

Why would these decision-makers decide in your favor? What is their need? What's their individual dynamic?

Who are the "antibodies" (opposing forces) involved in the decision-making? Who are the "probiotics"?

Who are the decision-influencers? Do you have relationships with them?

Is there a certain date by which a decision has to be made? How does your strategy line up with the date?

What are the organizations (if any) involved in the decision?

How will you know when key decision-makers have made their decision?

Strategy

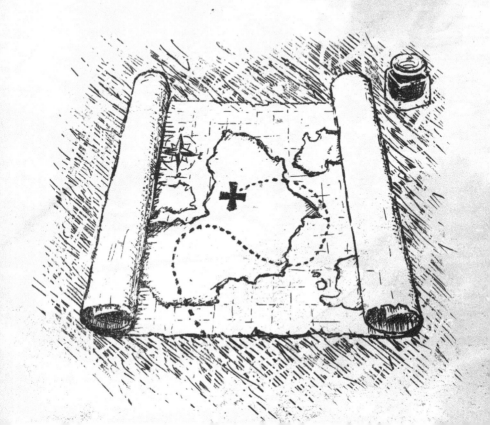

CHAPTER 9

STEP 4: DEVISE YOUR STRATEGIES

Life is like a giant chessboard—start playing.

THINK ABOUT THESE TERMS WHEN CONSIDERING STRATEGY

Approach, Blueprint, Design, Game Plan, Program, Game, Conduct, Stratagem, Treatment, Course of Action, Scenario

Once you understand your context and you've mapped your process, you can build a strategy—your roadmap for how you're going to get things done. Make it dynamic, filled with speed bumps and predicted traffic jams, so you can take all possibilities into account.

Consider a man you might not have heard of, but whose

legacy endures: Filippo Brunelleschi. Born in Florence in 1377, Brunelleschi moved to Rome in his twenties, where he spent ten years studying the ancient ruins, particularly focused on the Pantheon. At the time, no one knew how to create a self-supporting dome, so the ancient Roman structure enthralled Brunelleschi.

After years of research, he returned to Florence and entered a competition to design the Florence Cathedral dome, commissioned in part by, of course, the Medici family. His strategy to convince cathedral authorities of his brilliance involved standing an egg upright and cracking its bottom. They weren't entirely convinced, but it worked.

To build the dome itself, he had to continue developing new strategies, including inventing the world's first reverse gear, which allowed an ox to lower or raise a load with a simple switch. He also ensured there were minimal accidents—and therefore, minimal issues with authorities—by watering down his workers' wine to keep them sober. He had no formal training, and perhaps because he was unbound by traditional rules, he became the first true engineer of the Renaissance, employing highly effective, creative strategies to create an architectural masterpiece that adorns the Florentine skyline to this day.[16]

---

16 Devillier Donegan Enterprises. "Filippo Brunelleschi." PBS.org, accessed December 19, 2018. https://www.pbs.org/empires/medici/renaissance/brunelleschi.html.

A company I ran had an objective to pass legislation to fix a problem with pensions for our employees. Though we had a strategy in place, the team didn't have a clear understanding of the legislative process or the idiosyncratic, negative relationship between the governor and the mayor of the city in which we operated. As a result, we failed to meet our objective and fix the problem.

Rather than continue to hit our heads against a brick wall, we decided to step back, reassess our approach, and create a better strategy. We pivoted to focus entirely on the city, solving our problem via mayoral action rather than state government action. The point is, our strategy was dynamic enough that we could take all options into consideration and adjust accordingly.

If the mayor had responded to us negatively, we had contingencies in our strategies to create what would have amounted to an adversarial approach. Obviously, we preferred a collaborative one, but because of the time frame and map we put out there, we had to be ready for both at the same time.

Remember, strategy is always a dynamic process. Choose a direction but maintain flexibility to deal with the unexpected as you progress toward your objective. Your mixed table can help you plan and prepare for unexpected obstacles, enabling you to work this flexibility into your strategy long before you begin to execute.

STRATEGY WITHOUT CONTEXT

I learned the hard way what happens when you develop a strategy without understanding the context, and it cost me dearly. In the mid-2000s, during the wars in Iraq and Afghanistan, RL Leaders created a device called the Improvised Explosive Device Battle Drill (IEDBD) to train troops, which I mentioned in chapter 1. The military was losing many soldiers to IEDs at the time, and leaders had identified the first hundred days of deployment as the most dangerous.

General William S. Wallace, a four-star general in charge of TRADOC (United States Army Training and Doctrine Command), wanted to create a training simulator that allowed soldiers to feel the effects of an IED blast without getting hurt so they knew what to expect. He assigned the work to an organization within the Department of Defense called JIEDDO (Joint IED Defeat Organization), and JIEDDO officials elaborated on the idea and approached my company.

"We want a trainer that meets General Wallace's goals but also trains soldiers to watch out for enemy TTPs [Tactics,

Techniques, and Procedures], the telltale signs they leave behind when they've planted an IED."

We accepted the assignment and built an amazing simulation system that was a venerable mixed table in and of itself. We brought in Hollywood writers (thank you, Bob!) who created the storyboard in conjunction with subject-matter experts from the army and marines who had experienced blasts and had significant knowledge of the devices; a director of photography who helped develop a new camera system for us that could shoot in 360 without a shadow (before that was done); special-effects houses to help stitch it all together without warping; a theme-park ride provider to engineer it, bend the metal, and build the physical unit; retired army trainers to run the system; a wonderful producer to put it all together; and a host of others to integrate everything.

We built the simulation system inside a trailer that could be placed "down range," meaning they could take it to Afghanistan or anywhere else in the world. When the trailer was open, it contained a curved screen that was twenty-five-feet across and ten-feet high. There was a Humvee in the middle of it that rode on a six-degree motion platform that we could detonate from 2 g to 8 g.

It was perhaps the most realistic trainer ever built for ground forces. Instead of using computer graphics, we created an eight-camera system to film real footage for our 270-degree curved screen and the first 4K super-high-definition simulation system. The subcontracted theme-park designers we hired even helped us make it a fully immersive simulation. This included a 4-D soundscape that reproduced the "ringing in the ears" sensation after the simulated blast.

When an army general came to inspect it, he was astonished. Given his line of work, he'd been around real Humvees for years. Even so, as he walked around the trainer and placed his hands on it to feel the vibration, he asked us, "This is great, but what do you do with the exhaust?"

"There is no exhaust, General," I replied. "This is Hollywood. It's all special effects."

The soldiers who tested it gave it incredibly high marks. When we asked if they would recommend it to fellow soldiers, 95 percent said they would recommend it enthusiastically. Reviews were off the chart. I'd never seen anything like it.

Unfortunately, we'd failed to understand the context. We had a strategy to build a cutting-edge simulation system, it was heralded by the people who tested it, and praised by the military leaders who funded it. We planned to install one in every major military installation around the world. But the project was a failure.

During our process, we believed the technology would stand on its own, so we didn't develop the trainer to the army's specific requirements. We went well beyond the dramatically simpler version they'd asked for. We also failed to consider the context of the relationship between JIEDDO and the army. At the time, the vast majority of the leadership of JIEDDO were Army personnel, with a three-star general in charge and a one-star general as deputy director.

However, JIEDDO was a creation of the Office of the Secretary of Defense (OSD), created specifically to address the IED problem. From a budget standpoint, the army resisted the projects that came out of JIEDDO, because JIEDDO tended to build expensive pieces of technology and equipment that the army had not budgeted for.[17]

Metaphorically, JIEDDO would say, "Here you go. Here's a great tool that we've developed to battle IEDs. Now you need to go buy it."

The army would generally respond, "Thank you very

---

17 Lyle M. Dawley, Major, Lenore A. Marentette, Major, A. Marie Long, Captain, *Developing a Decision Model for Joint Improvised Explosive Device Defeat Organization (JIEDDO) Proposal Selection*, Wright-Patterson Air Force Base: Department of the Air Force, June 2008, http://www.dtic.mil/dtic/tr/fulltext/u2/a484369.pdf.

much. We've developed our own tools, and our budget is not capable of supporting this new equipment."

This dynamic played itself out over and over again with the big army and JIEDDO, ultimately, for all intents and purposes, leading to the collapse of JIEDDO as it used to be.

When we started working with JIEDDO, they were a relatively new organization, and they provided full funding for our initial simulator. We had an experienced team that included retired generals and colonels, a command sergeant major, and other great military experts. The end result was an extraordinarily effective simulation trainer for ground troops, but the army didn't want to buy them. We were unsuccessful in deploying them broadly because of the ongoing bureaucratic war between the army and JIEDDO.

Not understanding the context in building our strategy not only cost my company the contract, but more importantly, it cost soldiers the opportunity to train on what was arguably the most robust training device related to IEDs ever built.

THE IMPORTANCE OF NONVERBAL CUES

When devising your strategy, try to include some face-to-face time. In the digital age, it's more challenging than ever, but it's also vitally important. According to a landmark 1967 study in the *Journal of Consulting Psychology*, 93 percent of all communication is nonverbal. This includes everything from body language to tone of voice.[18] Though that exact percentage has been challenged over the years, the point is still relevant: when you fail to communicate face-to-face, you leave more room to be misunderstood by your audience.

The idiosyncratic behavior of human beings matters, so you need to be able to read the room to develop the strategy. In any given conversation, without nonverbal cues, it's harder to tell if the person you're talking to is being sarcastic, if she has the flu, if he just had a fight with his spouse, if she's dealing with a death in the family, or if he or she is enduring some other hardship. When you speak to someone face-to-face, you can often pick up on these things. For example, you might notice someone looks like he's feeling under the weather, which could explain his tone of voice and why he's not responding well to your sales pitch.

DIVERSIFY YOUR EXPERTISE

By the time you've finished developing your strategy, you

18   A. Mehrabian and S. R. Ferris, "Inference of Attitudes from Nonverbal Communication in Two Channels," *Journal of Consulting Psychology* 31, no. 3 (1967): 248–52.

should have decided who belongs on your team, and the context of your campaign should inform who you need working with you.

For example, if it's an external campaign, you might need a communications specialist. For a safety campaign, you probably need a safety manager or a training educator. Reserve the right to add people to the team as you become aware of needs. Halfway down the road, you might say, "Hey, you know what we still need? A marketing expert. Let's send for Deb and make a place for her at the table." There's nothing wrong with adapting as you go.

Even with the best strategy, the success of executing it falls largely on having the right team members, so think very carefully about who you need.

Curve Ball

PIVOTING YOUR STRATEGY

There are times when you have to pivot your strategy, which I've had to do throughout my career. Life is complicated. No situation is ever completely clean. There are going to be times when you've chosen one strategy and you're on the precipice of success, only to have the whole situation blow up in your face. Suddenly, you're all the way back at the beginning. If this happens, just remember, it's not the end of the world. Simply reassess your situation, remap your context, and adopt a new strategy to get to your objective.

When I was the interim CEO of MV Transportation, we had a strategy focused on a specific state capital from which we were looking for a certain outcome. We failed there, so we pivoted, instead focusing on a large municipality's city hall and local policymakers. In other words: same outcome, different strategy.

In both the Michael J. Fox campaign and the MV Transportation experience, having a flexible strategy allowed us to adjust to changing situations so we could react dynamically. We were fortunate in both instances that we had clear embarkation points for carrying out our strategy.

Strategy is ultimately all about the outcome. You create a process to get you to your objective, and if that path needs to evolve, so be it. As long as you wind up where you want to go, there's nothing wrong with reassessment and redirection. It might take twenty-seven different tries to obtain your goal, but if it's important to you, keep evolving your strategy until you get there.

Too often, people fail to achieve their objectives because they give up. If your strategy isn't working, change it and keep changing it until you make progress. Don't simply throw in the towel.

Perhaps you've worked to win an account for years only to have your boss reassign you. Don't give up. Will it through. Adopt another strategy that will realign you with your path. Usually, the situation is subtler than that, but a few complications or curveballs can rob you of your clarity. This is why constant feedback is important, to keep you consistently mindful of changes between your strategy and the context.

A good strategist ensures that there is harmony among strategy, tactics, process, and context so you never lose sight of the desired outcome. Always keep your objective in mind. Always remind yourself of what you're trying to achieve, and continually track where you are in relation to that objective so you know when you've arrived.

YOUR MORAL COMPASS

Sometimes, the line between right and wrong can get a little blurry, and as with everything in life, we have to check in with our morals when devising a campaign strategy.

I always ask myself, "Is this the right thing to do?"

Or rather, is this what Lee Atwater would do? If the answer is yes, I run in the opposite direction. Atwater was the brilliant political strategist who ran Ronald Reagan's aggressive 1980 presidential campaign and became infamous for using morally questionable techniques such as fake surveys and mailing scare letters to voters. Later in life, he expressed regret over many of the statements and strategies he used during the campaign. He crossed his own moral line and paid a price for it with a damaged reputation.

His story provides a note of caution. Just because we know how to achieve a goal doesn't mean we should. Let's not be Atwater. Let's ensure that our campaign strategies and objectives never cross those lines.

The bottom line is trust your gut. If it feels wrong, it probably is. Just ask yourself, "Is this the right thing to do?"

LAND MINES IN THE CREATION OF STRATEGY

Strategy doesn't unfold in a vacuum. We have to contend with land mines, and if we're not careful, these land mines can jeopardize the whole endeavor.

The first land mine is the context itself. The second land mine is not understanding the process. Creating and attempting to pursue a strategy without understanding these components is a recipe for disaster.

The third land mine is lack of focus. In his book *Outwitting the Devil*, Napoleon Hill says that 98 percent of people just drift through life, reacting to situations, and ultimately fail to achieve any meaningful success. The other 2 percent think clearly and confidently about the steps they need to take to achieve their goals, and then they *do the hard work*. If someone lacks the tenacity to keep making progress, they probably won't arrive at their objective.

A fourth land mine is failing to create a feedback loop between your context and strategy so you can track your progress.

Perhaps the greatest land mines of all are the ones that life throws at you on a daily basis. These external factors, the constant barrage of incoming, are capable of throwing any of us off our stride at any moment.

That is the paradox. Those very external forces are why we need to take the time to think holistically, develop a strategy, and run a campaign. That's what the most successful leaders do, which is a big part of *why* they are so successful.

Those who don't take that path, who let their days become disrupted by incoming, are most likely to fall victim to the dangers of distraction or groupthink. Think about it. It's difficult to carve out the space for deeper thinking, as the day-to-day work alone can be incredibly demanding. It's all the more reason that you step back and think holistically.

Social scientists have conducted a variety of studies on military decision-making during the Vietnam War and discovered that the prevailing fear that led the United States into war was a belief that if Vietnam fell to communism, it would lead to a domino effect. In strategy meetings, people continued to reinforce this idea. No one could seem to think past it.

Similarly, I suspect groupthink influenced President George W. Bush administration's decision to go to war in Iraq. Bush's advisors and strategists were convinced that Iraq had chemical weapons, and no amount of intelligence suggesting otherwise was going to make a difference. Contrary voices simply weren't heard or were actively opposed.

To avoid groupthink, always pay attention to the minority voice at the table. When one person deviates passionately from the consensus, pay attention. Give his or her opinion the benefit of real intellectual consideration. You never know where the proposed line of thinking might lead. It could very well protect you from a dangerous groupthink that will convince the rest of your team to commit to a bad strategy.

When everyone agrees, you run the risk of lulling one another into a false sense of security, but if you give contrary viewpoints real consideration, you are more likely to reach a place of true harmony. That's when you know you've developed a good strategy. You've considered multiple perspectives and potential problems, aligned the strategy with your context, set your sights on your objective, and prepared yourself to select tactics to carry out that strategy.

DEVISING YOUR STRATEGY

What kind of campaign are you running?

Virtually all strategies require a message, and a message requires storytelling. What's the message and story you want to convey?

How are you going to achieve your objectives at a higher level? If it's a political campaign, are you going negative or will you take the high road?

How many people do you need to influence to reach your objective?

Is your approach collaborative or adversarial? What are the outside influences that determine your approach? What are the internal influences?

Is there a shared understanding of the objective, or do you need to evangelize and educate?

What are the resources you can apply to the solution? Are you doing this on a shoestring budget, or do you have access to deep pockets? Are you somewhere in the middle?

What's your expectation on a timeline? What actions, responses, and inputs do you need to see to make sure you're on track? What are the milestones?

If strategy A fails, do you have a strategy B to fall back on?

Tactics

CHAPTER 10

STEP 5: BUILD YOUR TACTICS

Put the strongest arrows in your quiver.

**THINK ABOUT THESE TERMS
WHEN CONSIDERING TACTICS**

Arrows in a Quiver, Toolbox, Tool Kit, Means, Techniques, Nuts and Bolts, Ways and Methods, the Book

A well-thought-out campaign should look like a funnel with your objective at the slender end. Over time, the funnel narrows as you move closer to your goal. But how do you get there? By deploying tactics that move you down that funnel over time.

Tactics are the tools we use, the arrows in our quiver, to confront problems and advance toward our objectives—

and we can't implement a strategy without them. Put another way, tactics are the muscles that fill out the skeletal frame of your strategy.

When Leonardo da Vinci went to work for Ludovico Sforza, regent of Milan, he employed quite a bold tactic: he wrote a letter to the regent detailing his brilliance, vowing to prove his engineering and artistic skills were superior to his peers, with claims such as, "I can execute sculpture in marble, bronze, or clay, and also painting, in which my work will stand comparison with that of anyone else whoever he may be."[19] Sometimes, simply asking for a position in a confident manner is the best tactic. Sometimes not. It depends on the situation.

The range of tactics at your disposal today is incredible, so choose wisely and have a team that can execute all of them well. Most campaigns require a multitude of tactics; part of the art of running a campaign is discerning which tools are at your disposal and how you intend to wield them. Multidisciplinary teams are often necessary to execute complex campaigns.

Before you can assemble the team to deliver those tactics, spend additional time building out that funnel. Given the myriad factors at play, knowing where to start is half

---

19   Michael J. Gelb, *How to Think Like Leonardo da Vinci* (New York: Delacorte Press, 1998), 22.

the battle. In my experience, creating a schedule for your campaign is the ideal starting place.

MILESTONES ON YOUR PATH

To repeat the oft-used phrase, "What gets scheduled gets done." Scheduling your strategy is your first and most important tool. People resist it, but it drives action. Anything that needs to be done to reach your objective needs to be scheduled, and I recommend creating both a team schedule and personal schedules for team members.

There's an art to scheduling. To do it right, you need both "drivers" and "fillers." Drivers are the essential actions that must be done to move the compass needle. Fillers are tangential: actions that will take place but aren't absolutely necessary. Put them both on the schedule, but clarify the drivers to maximize efficiency. A schedule should contain important milestones on the path to the objective, with some sense of when you expect to arrive at each one. Line these milestones up with your drivers to create a clear line of action.

It also simply helps people maintain *focus*. It constantly clarifies where you and your team should spend most of your time and energy. In one of the organizations I worked with, I was shocked at the lack of control on the schedule. Everything was treated as "urgent," and very little prioritization took place. I believe this is a problem many organizations face. One of the first things I did as interim CEO of MV Transportation was to correct the schedule by approaching various stakeholders to determine our true priorities.

Once you've set your priorities, keep them front and center at all times, along with your objective. Your team members need a constant reminder of what you're attempting to accomplish. For example, if your campaign is a safety initiative at your company, your focus should be meeting with the safety team, communicating with relevant stakeholders on the insurance side, and relaying the importance of safety to your managers with clarity and consistency.

When creating your schedule, begin internally. What needs to be done within your organization in order to reach your objective? From there, build an external schedule. Again, this is your best hope of ensuring that your strategy is consistently carried out.

CHALLENGES TODAY

The adage in marketing used to be, "You have to let people know you exist."

With the advent of technology, that challenge has become

infinitely more complex. Advanced tech has helped broaden communication platforms, but it has also weakened the individual voice, curating a culture of clutter and noise.

Organizations and individuals alike have more communication platforms available to them than ever before, a reality that makes it harder—not easier—to communicate the right message to the right audiences. The implications of that simple truth are profound in campaigns, particularly of the external macro variety.

In order to reach your objectives in an external macro campaign, you almost certainly need to target a specific message to a specific audience in a manner that ensures that they hear it and act on it. Your audience is bombarded by a thousand different messages all the time, so one-time tactics that make you stand out for a moment may not help you achieve your long-term objective. Let's look at an example.

A BAD TACTIC

When I was deputy assistant to the secretary of defense, I got called to a meeting with Senator Krueger in the Hart Senate Office Building. I'm a simple man, so rather than bring an aide with me, I went to the meeting by myself. The senator wanted to talk about something called the

Defense Finance and Accounting Service (DFAS), which was an agency being established by the Department of Defense to reduce the costs of financial management and operations. When I walked into his office, I saw that it was packed with people, which wasn't an unusual occurrence, but the crowd was comprised of many of his constituents and a lot of media people with cameras.

"Hi," I said, walking into the room. "I'm John Rogers, and I'm here to meet with the senator."

Immediately, everyone in the room froze, and the senator rushed toward me. TV cameras lit up, and the senator dropped to his knees in front of me.

"Mr. Secretary," he said, his hands clasped in front of him. "Mr. Secretary, we need DFAS in Lubbock, Texas!"

I was aghast. A US senator was on his knees, begging me for something, and I had no staff with me. It was just me, the senator, and thirty people waiting to see how I would respond. I put my hand under his arm and tried to pick him up as he made his pitch.

He basically sandbagged me into coming to his office so he could put on a show for the media, demonstrating to his constituents that he was willing to get on his hands and knees in front of a young deputy assistant secretary of defense to bring DFAS to Texas.

In retrospect, it was a fascinating tactic that I'm sure made for a good clip on the local news back home that night, but the senator failed to understand the context. I wasn't the right decision-maker, and his little show mortified me. It didn't help his cause, and the DFAS agency wound up in a big facility outside of Cleveland.

GETTING IT RIGHT

Remember, ideas are the easy part. It's bringing them to bear in a way that affects change that's hard. The potential to one day apply this construct to your own campaigns means the possible industries, verticals, organization types, and objectives (much less the strategies and tactics) are exponential. To help you get this right, we're going to baseline our look at tactics against political campaigns.

Crazy, infuriating, and unending though they may be, large political campaigns offer a great window into the full range of campaign tactics and how the funnel should look.

For one thing, political campaigns do have an end date, and the tactics you deploy in the closing days are a hell of a lot narrower and more focused than they are at the beginning.

To give you an example of the granular nature of tactics, I reached out to Joe Zepecki, a friend and colleague who has worked on scores of political campaigns. He now applies his expertise to clients in both the corporate and public-affairs spaces. I wanted to get his take on a list of common, modern-day political campaign tactics instructive outside of the political arena. He broke those tactics down into six groups and explained why they merit understanding outside of the political realm. As you can see, when you delve into tactics, they become highly specific by nature.

1. **Mass Communication.** Ultimately, campaigns require communicating. The means by which you can mass communicate today are innumerable, if you're willing to pay to do so. Anytime you deliver the same content or communication to large-scale audiences, you're engaging in mass communication.

2. **Micro Communication.** Increasingly, campaigns can (and do) target unique messages to audiences of one. In short, when you use available data or information to communicate a personalized message to an individual, no matter the method, you are engaging in micro communication.

3. **Digital Communication.** Finally, because of the explosion in digital and its utility in both macro *and* micro communication, digital deserves its own bucket. If you're communicating via the internet or to a mobile device, you've gone digital.

4. **Earned Media.** And while the role of the Fourth Estate in the political world can seem a little twisted these days, "earning" media coverage in the press means something is being communicated to an external audience through the filter or lens of journalism, whether you're a Fortune 500 CEO or a candidate for the local school board.

5. **Fund-Raise.** When running for office, you fundraise to pay for your campaign. In the private sector, the source of the funds may be different, but you still have to get the dollars to spend in pursuit of your objective. Sometimes, raising money from outside sources is absolutely central to your campaign. Think capital campaigns for infrastructure development in the non-profit/charitable world.

6. **Political.** In political campaigns, we seek to win support from organizations and individuals that communicate things like credibility and values to others whose support we haven't won yet. In reality, what we're talking about are third-party validators or opinion leaders outside of politics who shape decision-making just as much as (if not more than) those inside the political world.

DIGGING DEEPER

Inside those types (or buckets) of tactics are actual individual tactics themselves. You may use some or all of these in your own campaigns. The only certainty is that using none of them means you've never run an external campaign.

Remember, while presented from the context of a political campaign, every one of these tactics is ultimately geared toward delivering the right message to the right target audience and can be adapted for your own use outside of politics.

- **Mass Communication:**
  - **Television Advertising.** For broadcast and cable, you're fighting for one gross ratings point at a time. Live viewership of television is in decline, leading to a disruption of this practice. "Event" television remains prize real estate—think big sporting events or networks doing live stage productions of classics.
  - **Radio Advertising.** This is done spot by spot, but it's another medium in decline.
  - **Outdoor/Transit.** This includes billboards, subway, and bus benches or interiors, and vehicle wraps.
  - **Direct Mail.** Capitalizing on bulk postage rates to deliver printed materials into the mailboxes of geographically based target audiences.

- ◦ **Robo-Calls.** Automated messages delivered to large-scale target audiences via telephone.
- ◦ **Guerilla Ads.** This includes everything from leafleting cars to chalking sidewalks outside major events, putting up yard signs and bumper stickers, or flying blimps or planes overhead with messages.
- **Micro Communication:**
  - ◦ **Canvassing.** Door-to-door communication. It's tough, so good shoe leather is recommended.
  - ◦ **Television Advertising.** It is now possible, in some cases, to target individual television boxes house by house in order to deliver different ads to different homes, determined by micro targeting.
  - ◦ **Direct Mail.** It is also possible to customize direct mail pieces at the household level, from personalized touches to variable data such as voting history or the names and addresses of neighbors in a "social pressure" mail campaign.
- **Digital Communication:**
  - ◦ **Email.** Email communication must have a call to action, directing the target audience to do something and explaining why.
  - ◦ **Texting.** This is growing in popularity, particularly around "get out the vote" efforts, though local campaigns are also using them for persuasion purposes.
  - ◦ **Video Advertising.** Streaming entertainment services offer paid placement, as does YouTube,

with options for pre-roll or mid-roll (though mid-roll costs more because it's more effective). You can also display video ads in social media feeds.

- ○ **Audio Advertising.** These are the online/digital version of radio ads, using streaming services such as Pandora and Spotify.
- ○ **Paid Search.** Driving traffic based on searches you identify and bid on.
- ○ **SEO.** Search engine optimization includes strategies for ensuring that your web pages are tagged and indexed correctly to appear in organic searches.
- ○ **Websites.** Obviously, everyone and every organization has a website these days, but you also still see many microsites used to generate traffic, sign-ups, or earned media.
- ○ **Social Media (Organic).** Content on your own social media feeds that is distributed algorithmically to your followers or likes; this can be static, video, display, or imagery. The hope is always to "go viral."
- ○ **Social Media (Paid).** Content on social media feeds delivered to targeted audiences. The current hot trend is serving content directly to an audience you have identified, as well as utilizing "lookalike audiences" that find targets you didn't know about.
- · **Earned Media:**

- **Opinion Editorials/Columns.** Writing in your own voice to lay out an argument in support of your campaign.
- **Interviews.** Delivering your campaign message in a format where a single journalist asks the questions. These are usually done in person but can be done virtually.
- **Press Conference/Gaggle/Media Availability.** Delivering your campaign message in a format where multiple journalists have an opportunity to ask you questions. This can also be done in person or virtually.
- **Press Releases.** Written information delivered to reporters via email with select information and content.
- **Events.** Inviting the news media to cover a real-world event, which could range from a large-scale rally in an arena to a solemn speech on a given topic or a quiet visit between a candidate and an individual or family in their home.
- **Rapid Response.** Seizing on breaking news to quickly insert your campaign message into developing stories.
- **Oppo Drops.** Packaging and delivering negative information ("opposition research") about your opponent into a digestible format for a journalist to turn into a news story.
- **Crisis Communications.** Responding to damag-

ing information about your campaign quickly—the inverse of rapid response or an oppo drop.

- **Fund-Raising:**
  - **Events.** These range from low-dollar affairs that double as opportunities to recruit and sign up volunteers to high-dollar galas that can add six figures to your campaign account in the course of an evening.
  - **Direct Mail.** Fund-raising direct mail typically lands in the "middle" zone of solicitations/contributions ($100 to $500) and doubles as an opportunity to deliver your message.
  - **Online.** The majority of online fund-raising continues to be via email, with highly targeted asks (based on past contribution history matched to email), typically of less than $50. Campaigns often use traditional sales tactics to make low-dollar donations seem more impactful. For example, "matching" campaigns are a frequently used tactic that allows supporters to double their impact by having small-dollar contributions matched by a large donor. "Direct donate" ads are an emerging tactic that allow visitors to social media pages and websites to go directly to a secure location where an online donation can be made.
  - **Call Time.** This means picking up the phone, dialing a number, and asking for financial support. Rinse and repeat.

- **Bundling.** Influencers and opinion leaders will "bundle" contributions from like-minded individuals, often from the same industry.
- **Political:**
  - **Endorsements.** Formal endorsements from organizations and institutions or prominent individuals, who are referred to as "third-party validators" in nonpolitical lexicon.
  - **Coalition Building.** This is frequently used to illustrate support among a key demographic or interest group: "Business Leaders for X," "Women for Y," or "African Americans for Z."

As Zepecki's list indicates, political campaigns use various forms of media internally, externally, both paid and earned. Paid media primarily refers to advertising, and earned media refers to public relations. People running political campaigns work hard to maintain consistency in all forms of messaging, viewing both paid and earned media holistically; regardless of the medium, inconsistent messaging is the fastest way to lose voters. If someone runs a pro-Second Amendment campaign, putting out a press release opposing gun ownership would devastate your perceived authenticity.

When selecting which tactics are right for your campaign, analyze available data. Identify your target audience and determine the best way to reach them.

Tactics are simply strategy brought to life. Think of strategy as what gives shape, and tactics as what creates motion. Each of your tactics helps you accomplish some mini goal that moves you closer to your objective.

Every campaign, whether political, military, corporate, or otherwise, will operate in a similar fashion. In each case, it requires a series of tactical steps to support a logical sequence of events that propels people down the funnel toward their objectives. Military strategists are trained to do this, but it's the same basic approach that every campaign must embrace.

AVOIDING BLIND SPOTS

One mistake many organizations and leaders make is failing to take advantage of all the tactics at their disposal. We can all develop blind spots that hinder us from seeing fantastic tactics. Fortunately, mixed tables are made in part to counteract this, as they often provide greater creativity in identifying tactics for executing a strategy.

During my campaign on stem cells, I was a member of the Coalition for the Advancement of Medical Research (CAMR), comprised of over a hundred different organizations advocating for embryonic stem cell research. They had great advocacy within Washington, DC, but in lobbying Congress, they failed to incorporate certain tools at their disposal to influence electoral politics. In the absence of pressure from the electorate, policymakers were unwilling to move on the stem cell issue, even though CAMR technically had a majority of politicians on their side.

Seeing this need, I began to advocate passionately for getting involved in electoral politics, though CAMR was reluctant. Ultimately, this is the tactic that Michael J. Fox and I employed, passing our message to individual Senate races, which proved highly successful.

KEEP YOUR MIXED TABLE IN THE MIX

When selecting tactics to carry out your strategy, it's a good idea to assemble a few subject-matter experts. If you know, for instance, that you want to get a certain piece of legislation passed, political experts can advise you on how to approach this by helping you map out how to obtain funding when Congress is in session, how to influence the votes of individual politicians, and how to identify key champions within Congress who will push the issue.

If you are pursuing a marketing campaign, put a marketing team in place to conduct focus groups comprised of people from your target market. A mixed table including subject-matter experts can analyze the resulting data. Of course, as with any mixed table, it's optimal not to include *only* subject-matter experts from one specific industry. Add a few outside thought leaders as well to keep everyone sharp, and you will have a much better chance at avoiding some of the common narrow-minded pitfalls we all can stumble into when we're not careful.

In all of this, employ the broadest range of tactics available. Sometimes, we're faced with tactics we'd rather not use, and that's okay, as long as not using them is an active choice, not passive ignorance.

COMMON TACTICAL MISSTEPS

The first and greatest mistake one can make in selecting tactics is not being mindful of the schedule. Remember, nothing happens on its own. It takes hard work to make progress, and the way to make progress is to keep a schedule and stick to it.

The second mistake is failing to be thoughtful about the full array of tactics at your disposal. Da Vinci didn't have a great name or family to rely on, so he looked to his skills as a writer and charmer and used them to obtain work. Not being mindful is an easy mistake to make when you're already running ninety miles per hour trying to accomplish your objective. If you have a hard time determining what tactics are available, consider what others have done in similar campaigns. What tactics have they used? What tactic did they *fail to employ* that they should have?

If you're going too fast, I encourage you to take a deep breath, slow down, and spend some time being mindful. Pump the brakes, bring your team together in a room, and think through all of your available tactics.

Once you have your tactics in place, it's time to execute your campaign with discipline. In the next chapter, we'll take a look at what that means and how you can get started.

GATHER YOUR TOOLS

Most people don't use all of the tools available to them. Are you taking advantage of every available tool?

How are you going to communicate your message/ story? Are you utilizing media? If so, what media (social media, television, print)? Are you using third-party influencers? Which team members are delivering the message?

How will you make sure your message cuts through the clutter and stands out? How are you differentiating?

Is there a PR aspect to your campaign? If so, what is it?

Is there a legal aspect to your campaign? If so, what is it?

Is there a grassroots element to your campaign? If so, what is it?

Do you have resources for fund-raising?

What are the analytical, data-driven tools at your disposal, and how are you utilizing them? What are the nontraditional sources you can apply?

Execute with Discipline

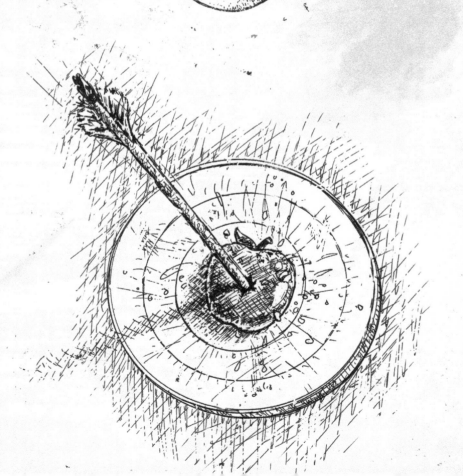

CHAPTER 11

STEP 6: EXECUTE WITH DISCIPLINE

Don't get in the way of yourself or your goals.

THINK ABOUT THESE TERMS WHEN CONSIDERING EXECUTION

Engagement, Performance, Act, Doing, Accomplishments, Finish, Implement, Enforce, Enact

Everything you've done so far has led you to the moment of execution. If you've made it to this point, congratulations. This is where it all tends to fall apart. Many great plans have been formulated but never realized. As a wise person once said, "Ideas are easy. Execution is the tough part."

We can have superb mixed tables, excellent campaign

plans, and still fail in the execution for one reason or another. However, with these tools, we're much more likely to find success.

Michelangelo completed the Sistine Chapel in a mere four years, an astonishing amount of time given the enormity of the project. His largest figures reach thirteen feet tall. How did he finish such a massive undertaking so quickly?

Succinctly, he had an exceptional campaign plan.

He never attempted to paint his figures freehand. He sketched them and then employed an artistic technique called pouncing, which involves pricking holes into the outline of the sketch, laying the sketch against the plaster, and then pressing charcoal against the holes. This transfers the sketch to the plaster.

When an aging Pope Julius II implored him to work more quickly so that he might see the completed version before his death, Michelangelo had to switch strategies to properly execute. He replaced the charcoal with a blade, allowing him to incise his sketches directly onto the plaster, which made for a much faster process.[20]

---

20 "How Did Michelangelo Complete the Sistine Chapel in Such a Short Time?" (video), *Smithsonian*, accessed September 20, 2018, https://www.smithsonianmag.com/videos/category/smithsonian-channel/pouncing-on-the-sistine-chapelpouncing-on-th/.

In the end, he completed the Sistine Chapel in 1512, just under four months before Pope Julius II's death, fulfilling the pope's wishes to see the finished chapel.

Michelangelo wasn't simply a talented painter and sculptor. He was a gifted creator, able to devise variant strategies and tactics when needed, allowing him to execute and complete one of the most beloved, astounding pieces of art our world has yet seen.

Ideally, what I've outlined in the previous chapters will help you execute more efficiently and with an informed outlook. You've crystallized your objective, clarified the context, mapped the process, crafted a strategy, and selected a wide array of tools. You know what needs to happen and when it needs to happen.

Now, it's time to execute.

YOUR MOMENT OF TRUTH

Whether you're part of a football team executing a winning drive, the military waging a war on terror, or a business enacting a growth campaign, it all comes down to this moment. You have to take the first step and put the plan into action.

Your plan will help you deal with the fastballs, sliders, and curveballs, which will come fast and furious. Expect them, but don't let anxiety about the unexpected cause you to hesitate. If your plan is dynamic and flexible, you'll be able to handle them.

MILESTONES ON THE PATH

I recommend creating a timeline so you can set markers on the path to your objective. Know what your milestones are and when you need to reach each one—as you begin to execute your strategy, these milestones will help you track your progress.

This is true no matter what industry you're in, but you can clearly see this in a construction project. Good general contractors have brilliant project management skills that allow them to track milestones with finesse. If it's not your strong suit, you might need to use a calendar app or project management software to help you. The goal is to be certain you understand what your milestones are, so you can measure your progress toward them throughout your campaign.

Communication

COMMUNICATION, THE VERTICAL INTEGRATOR

People and organizations get tripped up because they lack internal communication channels and constant vigilance about the flow of information. There's a variety of ways you can address that. As you execute your campaign, remind yourself that communication is the vertical integrator *throughout* the campaign. It doesn't stop at tactics and will remain essential in the execution.

If you think about every component of the campaign we've discussed as horizontal, communication is the vertical, connecting them all. Feedback is key to execution and does not occur without communication. A great coach to a group of CEOs once explained that our roles— our *real* roles—were to foster effective communication. In other words, we're the communicators in chief. It's all about messaging. It's all about communication. Without it, execution cannot occur.

It starts with communication among team members; hearing regularly from each person helps you determine whether or not you're on track. As the old saying goes, "Bird-dogging is not badgering." It takes constant vigilance to ensure that the communication flow remains open and dynamic, constant vigilance to track every aspect of your campaign, and constant vigilance to execute every step of the campaign.

It's not that people intentionally fail to monitor their progress. They simply get distracted. More than ever, someone has to be the bird dog, keeping on top of every team member to propel progress.

This is as simple as consistently approaching team members and asking for an update: "Hey, Tristin, can you help me understand where you're at with X?"

I have a group of lobbyists working for me on a state effort right now, but I've been warned that if I don't stay on top of them, it won't happen. It's the same in most campaigns. Without regular communication, sharing information, and checking in with team members, it's easy to lose your way. Remember, all your team members deal with impediments coming at them from various directions. Without constant discipline and keeping people on track, your chances of success decline over time.

Fortunately, if you put in the early work to prepare your strategy, build your team, and select your tools, much of the plan will run itself. All you need to do is maintain a feedback loop among your objective, context, process, strategy, and tactics so you can see where you are.

It's not unlike baking a cake. To reach your objective, you first gather your ingredients: eggs, flour, sugar, baking powder. You measure each ingredient, mix them, and put the cake in the oven. Now, you get to sit back and watch it bake.

This is much better than spontaneously asking yourself, "What should I bake tonight? What ingredients do I have in the cupboard? Maybe I need to run to the store. Do I have the right measuring cups?" In that scenario, you are far less likely to successfully bake your cake. At best, it will certainly take longer and be a lot more frustrating.

To use a dramatically different example, taking out Osama bin Laden required a vast amount of careful planning. The desired outcome was obvious, but the preparation required deep and artful work. The US military created a facsimile of bin Laden's compound in Pakistan so they could rehearse their strategy based upon the latest intelligence. An admirable amount of mindful planning and training, combined with tactics that used the latest technology and military hardware, and constant logistical support throughout the execution phase, contributed to the ultimate success of that campaign.

The SEAL Team didn't fly into Pakistan by the seat of their pants. Every aspect of the strategy—and every tactic—was carefully considered, measured, and practiced. The execution was performed with precision, and the SEALs were equipped to contend with any unforeseen complications, resulting in a flawless, disciplined campaign.

THE DANGER OF DISTRACTION

Finances often become a major source of distraction during the execution phase of a campaign. Of course, most objectives have some sort of financials tied to them, but sometimes meeting the numbers becomes its own objective. Leaders find it difficult to relax when they feel constant financial pressure.

Many campaigns require a large investment in the short term, which needs a strategy of its own. The danger is that the short-term burden becomes a diversion for leaders, so they stop focusing on the long-term objective. In numerous corporations, leaders become so fixated on quarter-to-quarter results that they can't think and plan for bigger goals further down the road.

As you begin to execute your campaign, I advise you to be careful not to allow short-term burdens to sideline your team. Keep your focus on the end goal.

Every organization struggles to work on what's just around the corner while still meeting long-term goals. In *Forbes* magazine, Victor Lipman discusses how 48 percent of CEOs struggle to find time for self-reflection.

As he contends, "With too much to do in too little time, finding reflective time for yourself is a challenge for management at all levels."[21] This is the tension that causes many campaigns to fail. It's the reason why so few of the companies that were on the Fortune 500 list in 1955, or even 1996, remain. They were too fixated on what was just around the corner and failed to plan or execute long-term strategies.

My partner Brian often says, "Organizations are on the path toward failure," because they lose track of their overall objective. The short-term stress and strain of shareholder demands and financial burdens pull leaders off track.

Financials aren't the only distraction, of course. We confront unforeseen events all the time. Sometimes, we can use them to our advantage. When Rush Limbaugh mocked Michael J. Fox, we used it to our benefit, turning stem cell research from a niche issue into a deciding factor in the 2006 Senate race. More often than not, the unanticipated becomes a series of dangerous distractions that derail the whole campaign. People scramble to deal with sudden problems and lose sight of their ultimate outcome.

---

21   Victor Lipman, "What Do CEOs Find Unexpectedly Hard?" *Forbes*, September 3, 2018, https://www.forbes.com/sites/victorlipman/2018/09/03/what-do-ceos-find-unexpectedly-hard.

If you expect and plan for the surprises, short-term financial burdens, and distractions, and keep your focus on your overall outcome at all times, you'll be far more likely to get there. You've already gathered the ingredients, carefully measured them, mixed them, and put them in the oven. Now, as the cake bakes, remember to keep a watchful eye.

QUESTIONS FOR EXECUTION

Have you created a calendar with milestones so you can keep track of your progress?

What actions in the campaign can you gut or put on cruise control?

CONCLUSION

I believe life is meant to be lived large, but in order to do so, we need tools. We need structure. In the first part of this book, I've hopefully provided you with a means for dreaming bigger, confronting greater obstacles than you thought you could, and reaching further than you previously dared through the power of mixed tables and creativity.

We no longer live in the proverbial village of bygone times. Many still live in *literal* villages, but the societal expectation that an entire village congregates to accomplish objectives is a notion of the past. However, it's just as prevalent today as it was thousands of years ago.

It sounds so simple when broken down. We're bringing back the idea of working with people who possess a wide variety of skills and talents. We're bringing back the open-minded approach of the Renaissance. While we will never re-create that time period (and, to be honest, I'm quite happy with modern plumbing and electricity), the great thinkers of the fifteenth and sixteenth centuries were role models for a reason.

They didn't simply create, whether through art like Michelangelo and Shakespeare or by funding artists to actualize a vision like the Medici family. Their way of *thinking* helped change the world. Though incredibly gifted, da Vinci famously died having completed only seventeen paintings, some of which are incomplete, yet he continues to earn our admiration and respect because of the way his mind worked.[22]

If we were to embrace such holistic thinking, we could create our own Renaissance. As we face the continuous changes brought about by technology and our ever-evolving norms and mores, we need that mindset now more than ever.

Who knows what we could create in the world if everyone adopted this approach?

COPING WITH TODAY'S CHALLENGES

Every generation says life is more complicated today

22   Michael J. Gelb, *How to Think Like Leonardo da Vinci* (New York: Delacorte Press, 1998), 38.

than the previous generation. It also happens to be true. Studies indicate that consumers today are exposed to around ten thousand messages every day from various channels.[23]

Beyond that, there's the Collingridge dilemma, which postulates that technology advances in such a way that by the time it's finally developed, no one, not even the developers, can say what the ultimate effect will be on society. Put differently, technology develops faster than policymakers can keep up with it, let alone establish thoughtful rules or laws.

Imagine being in a position of leadership and facing that constantly. The mixed table, done correctly, at least allows that leader to think about and anticipate the future.

RUNNING CAMPAIGNS

In the second part of the book, I've attempted to illuminate a daily habit many of us are oblivious to: we run campaigns every day of our life, but do we run them effectively?

From ensuring that our objectives are manageable to

---

23 Joshua Saxon, "Why Your Customers' Attention Is the Scarcest Resource in 2017," *American Marketing Association,* accessed September 21, 2018, https://www.ama.org/partners/content/Pages/why-customers-attention-scarcest-resources-2017.aspx.

implementing a proper communication system among team members, being creative and flexible with strategies to drafting a concrete schedule and identifying key tactics, there are *so many tools* at our disposal to help us run campaigns. Using just one will help inch you along.

I'm not saying you can't succeed without a mixed-table and campaign approach. Organizations and individuals sometimes accomplish amazing feats by fumbling their way in the dark, but you don't have to. You don't have to run the risk of being among Napoleon Hill's 98 percent. If you only adopt one part of the approach I've laid out in this book, you'll be far more likely to land among the 2 percent. Still, employing the full range of tools will give you the greatest chance of success.

Naming and informing these processes will ideally provide you with a means for acting upon those dreams and ideas.

Whether you're dealing with national security, an organizational challenge, or parenting, the insights in this book can help. By examining a challenge in different ways, you can develop a more effective strategy and gather a wider array of tools. Your ensuing campaign will run more effectively, deal with the unexpected more efficiently, and carve a clearer path to your desired outcome.

INTO THE FUTURE

We're not in the midst of a Renaissance. We're not in our own version of the Middle Ages either. But we could slip into either one. How we proceed as a society will partially depend on how we evolve. There isn't time for limited thinking. We must be holistic and thoughtful, fostering a world that deals in creativity and civility, rather than narrow-mindedness and belligerence. The more holistic our thinking, the more we'll create, the more problems we'll solve, and the more we'll shape a world worthy of future generations.

Good luck, live long and prosper, and may the force be with you.

ACKNOWLEDGMENTS

Who don't I thank? That's a harder question because all of my friends and family have served as my guides and partners on this journey.

With that said, there are a few big shout-outs I'd like to make, starting with my daughter, Alex. Thank you for co-creating, editing, researching, writing, and getting me to open up. You have helped bring this book to life in ways I could never have dreamed of. You're amazing!

Diane and Mitch, thank you for making us both better, as well as your love and constant insights and humor.

Nancy, Vicki, and Lynn, you've made me better and I love you all, as I do our clan.

Joe, thank you for lending your great, broad knowledge on all facets of the book, but in particular, your lead on campaign tactics. You're awesome! Jen, thanks for your amazing shoulders and wonderful efforts in moving this all forward.

Richard, I love your superpowers and your willingness to share them with me. Thanks for lending your great perspectives and helping me think through my three words along with suggesting I write this book to begin with.

Kyle, Lauren, and Michael, thanks for the great work on the graphics!

Thanks to my partners and team members for pushing me, along with putting up with this book and me. Erik, after almost eighteen years, you deserve a special shout-out, if not a medal. It's been a joy! Dick, a shout-out to you, too, for helping improve the mixed-table effort and giving me rhino skin. Brian, thanks for making me wiser. Alan, thanks for making me kinder.

Thanks to all the LA creatives in my life—Greg, David, Rich, Tom, Bob, Kelly, Kristanna, Kent, Eric, Chris, Baz, Tom, Danny, and Chase—who have taught me so much about the West Coast.

On the East Coast: Ted, Larry, Mitchell, Alan, Christina, David, Gershon, Andy, Mike, Jerry, Mark, and Jolene, thank you for all that you do and have done.

Thank you MV family, particularly Alex, Feysan, Lisa, and Kevin.

Marc, this one's for you.

ABOUT THE AUTHOR

The three words that define **JOHN ROGERS** are *impact*, *insight*, and *integrity*. His worldview posits that most challenges can be solved by holistic thinking coupled with an effective HIGH-IMPACT campaign. The results of this approach speak for themselves and demonstrate the flexibility of Rogers's technique. From protecting twenty-thousand jobs in the mobility sector to bringing together the best minds in Hollywood and the national security community to reduce the risk of homegrown terrorism, Rogers's campaigns are defined by much more than simply achieving desired outcomes. They have made a difference in the world and can make a difference in your business or organization, too.

CPSIA information can be obtained
at www.ICGtesting.com
Printed in the USA
LVHW020056171219
640668LV00006B/82/P